Vogue® Knitting
Quick
Reference

THE ULTIMATE PORTABLE KNITTING COMPENDIUM
by the editors of *Vogue® Knitting Magazine*

Vogue® Knitting
Quick Reference

sixth&spring books

Vogue® Knitting
The Ultimate Knitting Book

Without the knowledge that came before us, this book and all the techniques included would not have been possible. The editors are indebted to the following: Barbara Walker, Elizabeth Zimmermann, Meg Swansen, Corinne Shields, Claudia Manley, Montse Stanley, Mary Thomas, Sally Harding, Margery Winter, Kaffe Fassett

Editorial Concept and Development
Lola Erlich

Art Director and Designer
Karen Salsgiver

Project Director
Martha Moran

Magazine Editors
Joni Coniglio, Carla S. Patrick, Nancy J. Thomas

Book Editor
Cherie Gillette

Illustrations
Kate Simunek, Chapman Bounford and Associates (UK)

Copy Editors
Debbie Conn, Liza Wolsky

Editorial Coordinator
Catherine Quartulli

Design Assistants
Susan Carabetta, Chi Ling Moy

Contributing Writers
Kaffe Fassett, Barbara Walker, Elizabeth Zimmermann, Margaret Bruzelius, Mari Lynn Civelek

Photography
Jack Deutsch

Contributors
Trevor Bounford, Berta Carela-Harkavy, Ann Clue, Carol Covington, Sandy Daniels, Roger Eaton, Lillian Esposito, Mary Ann Esposito, Elsie Faulconer, Maureen Fitzpatrick, David Frederickson, Joe Marc Freedman, Norah Gaughan, Kathy Grasso, Ilisha Helfman, Chris Jones, Sylvia Jorrin, Teri Leve, Hugh MacDonald, Elizabeth Malament, Nancy Marchant, Margarita Mejia, Annie Modesitt, Deborah Newton, Kay Niederlitz, Susan Olsen, Lisa Paul, Rose Ann Pollani, Dorothy Radigan, Mick Rivers, Cindy Rose, Emma Scott, Jessica Shatan, Karen Sisti, Joe Vior

Yarns and Tools
Westminster Trading Corp., Anny Blatt, Berger du Nord, Plymouth Yarns, Susan Bates, Inc., Boye Needle Co., Patternworks

Typesetting
The Sarabande Press

Separations
Acolortone Limited (UK)

Preparation and Film
Reflex Reprographics (UK)

Printer
Cayfosa Quebecor

Consultant, Book Publishing
Mike Shatzkin

Copyright ©2002 by Sixth&Spring Books

Library of Congress Cataloging-in-Publication Data

Vogue knitting quick reference : the ultimate portable knitting compendium / edited by Trisha Malcolm
    p. cm
    ISBN 1-931543-12-7 (spiral)
    1. Knitting. I. Malcolm, Trisha, 1960- II. Vogue knitting international.

TT820 . V6253 2002
746.43'2--dc21

2002021085

Manufactured in China

Vogue®Knitting Quick Reference

Editorial Director
Trisha Malcolm

Editor
Carla Scott

Sr. Art Director
Chi Ling Moy

Art Director
Marta M. Strait

Copy Editor
Betty Christiansen

Editorial Assistant
Cathy Franklin

Manager, Book Division
Theresa McKeon

Production Manager
David Joinnides

President & Publisher
Art Joinnides

Co-Chairmen
Jay H. Stein
John E. Lehmann

CONTENTS

SPECIAL FEATURES OF THIS BOOK

Vogue® Knitting Quick Reference has been designed to provide knitters with the most-used knitting information from the classic *Vogue® Knitting* reference book in a compact, portable guide. The perfect size to slip in a knitting bag, this book offers at-a-glance guidance on every step of completing a knitting project—from casting on and determining gauge to following knitting instructions, correcting errors, adding embellishments, and assembling your finished project. You'll find sections devoted to color knitting, knitting in the round, and finishing techniques as well as comprehensive lists of knitting abbreviations, terms, and internationally recognized symbols.

Vogue® Knitting Quick Reference incorporates the best features of *Vogue® Knitting* into its concise format. You'll find the same detailed instructions, clear illustrations, and helpful tip boxes. In addition, each chapter of this guide has been color-coded for easy reference—each one begins with a colored contents page that lists the techniques explained within that chapter, and coordinating bars at the bottom of each page offer handy references to section heads. The spiral binding of this guide allows it to lie flat in front of you, leaving your hands free to work as you follow instructions.

Techniques featured in *Vogue® Knitting Quick Reference* were selected to accommodate a range of knitting abilities. Wherever possible, variations on basic techniques have been included, resulting in a collection of instructions that serves beginning knitters and those with greater experience equally well. Whether practicing your first knitting stitches, searching for a creative alternative to a common technique, or simply looking for the answer to a question, *Vogue® Knitting Quick Reference* will provide you with thorough information, at a glance, wherever your knitting happens to take you.

I. Basic Techniques

Holding Yarn and Needles

Watch other people knit and you'll notice that everyone has a different way of holding the yarn and knitting needles. This is the most difficult thing to master when learning to knit, and it's important that you find a method that works for you.

The way you hold the yarn and needles will partly depend on which of two basic ways you choose to knit. If you use the English method, you hold the yarn in your right hand; with the Continental method, you hold it in your left.

Your own preferences will also affect your holding position. For example, you may find it easier to knit close to the tips of the needles, or you may prefer to work with the stitches farther back on the shafts. You may use only one finger to control the yarn, or you may use several fingers to obtain the same control. Any method is correct as long as the yarn flows evenly and the tension is consistent. Just work in the way that is easiest for you. Once you become comfortable with holding your needles, you will automatically increase your knitting speed.

Two traditional methods of holding yarn and needles are shown here.

English

1 Hold the needle with the stitches in your left hand as shown. Wrap the yarn around your little finger and then around the index finger on your right hand.

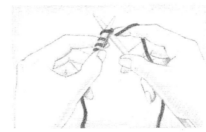

2a Hold the working needle with your right hand as shown, controlling the tension with your right index finger.

2b An alternate method is to place the working needle between the thumb and index finger of your right hand as if you were holding a pencil.

Continental

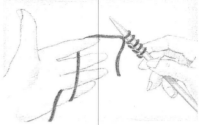

1 Hold the needle with the stitches in your right hand. Wrap the yarn around your little finger and then around the index finger of your left hand. Transfer the needle back to your left hand.

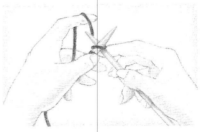

2 Hold the working needle with your right hand as shown, controlling the tension with your left index finger.

Casting On

Before you begin to knit, you must first make a foundation row called a cast-on. You can choose from a wide variety of cast-on methods, some worked with one needle and others with two. The methods presented here are basic, multipurpose cast-ons. You may want to try all methods, but if you are like most knitters, you will probably use one or two cast-ons for most purposes.

The cast-on row affects all the rows that follow, so it is essential to create the neatest edge possible. If you are a beginner, choose a basic cast-on and practice keeping the tension of the loops even before you begin to knit. If your cast-on stitches are too tight, you may have difficulty working the first row. Try casting on with two needles held together and removing one of them before you begin to knit, or try using a larger needle. If your cast-on stitches are too loose, the edge will stretch out. You can tighten your cast-on by using a smaller needle, then changing to the correct size on the first row.

Once the loops are on the needle, you must decide which will be the right and wrong side of your work. Many cast-on methods form a loopy edge on one side (much like that of a purl stitch), while the other side is flatter and smoother. Pick the one you like best. Make a mental note of whether the cast-on tail is on the right or left side of your work to help you keep track of right and wrong sides.

Slip Knot

The first stitch of any cast-on method is a slip knot. For both double cast-on methods, you must leave a predetermined length of yarn free before working the slip knot. A general guide is to allow a length of approximately three times the planned width of the cast-on edge. For the other methods, only an eight- to ten-inch (20–25cm) length is necessary.

1 Hold the short end of the yarn in your palm with your thumb. Wrap the yarn twice around the index and middle fingers.

2 Pull the strand attached to the ball through the loop between your two fingers, forming a new loop.

3 Place the new loop on the needle. Tighten the loop on the needle by pulling on both ends of the yarn to form the slip knot. You are now ready to begin one of the following cast-on methods.

DOUBLE CAST-ON

The double cast-on method provides a firm yet elastic edge and is frequently recommended for beginners.

1 Make a slip knot on the right needle, leaving a long tail. Wind the tail end around your left thumb, front to back. Wrap the yarn from the ball over your left index finger and secure the ends in your palm.

2 Insert the needle upward in the loop on your thumb. Then with the needle, draw the yarn from the ball through the loop to form a stitch.

3 Take your thumb out of the loop and tighten the loop on the needle. Continue in this way until all the stitches are cast on.

DOUBLE CAST-ON—THUMB METHOD

The thumb method has the same finished look as the double cast-on.

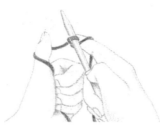

1 Make a slip knot on the right needle, leaving a long tail. Wind the tail end around your left thumb, front to back. Wrap the yarn from the ball over your right index finger and secure both strands in your palms.

2 Insert the needle upward through the loop on your thumb.

3 Using your right index finger, wrap the yarn from the ball over the needle knitwise. Pull the yarn through the loop on your thumb to form a stitch. Tighten the loop on the needle by pulling on the short end. Continue in this way until all the stitches are cast on.

Single cast-on

This is the simplest but not the neatest method of casting on. It is a good technique to use when teaching children.

1 Place a slip knot on the right needle, leaving a short tail. Wrap the yarn from the ball around your left thumb from front to back and secure it in your palm with your other fingers.

2 Insert the needle upward through the strand on your thumb.

3 Slip this loop from your thumb onto the needle, pulling the yarn from the ball to tighten it. Continue in this way until all the stitches are cast on.

Knitting-on

With the knitting-on method, use two needles and one length of yarn.

1 Make a slip knot on the left needle. *Insert the right needle knitwise into the stitch on the left needle. Wrap the yarn around the right needle as if to knit.

2 Draw the yarn through the first stitch to make a new stitch, but do not drop the stitch from the left needle.

3 Slip the new stitch to the left needle as shown. Repeat from the * until the required number of stitches is cast on.

CABLE CAST-ON

The cable cast-on forms a sturdy yet elastic edge. It is perfect for ribbed edges.

1 Cast on two stitches using the knitting-on cast-on described on page 5. *Insert the right needle between the two stitches on the left needle.

2 Wrap the yarn around the right needle as if to knit and pull the yarn through to make a new stitch.

3 Place the new stitch on the left needle as shown. Repeat from the *, always inserting the right needle in between the last two stitches on the left needle.

ALTERNATE CABLE CAST-ON

This cast-on creates a firm edge for knit one, purl one ribbing. After casting on, knit the knit stitches through the back loops on the first row only.

1 Cast on two stitches using the knitting-on method. *Insert the right needle from back to front between the two cast-on stitches.

2 Wrap the yarn around the left needle as if purling and pull the yarn through.

3 Place the new stitch on the left needle as shown. Cast on a new stitch using the cable cast-on. Repeat from the *, always inserting the right needle between the last two stitches on the left needle.

THE BASIC KNIT STITCH

The first stitch you will learn to make is called a knit stitch. You can work this stitch in two basic ways.

The most common technique in English-speaking countries is known as the English or American method. The second method, which has always been associated with European countries, is called the Continental or German method. Each has its merits.

If someone taught you to knit, you probably learned the method used by your teacher. If you are learning now, you can try both methods and decide which is best for you. Usually the first technique you learn will be the easiest for you. (If you learn both methods, however, you will be able to knit colorwork patterns using both hands.)

In the English method, your right hand controls the tension of the yarn and wraps it around the needle. The right needle usually rests on your lap or under your arm while you knit.

ENGLISH

1 Hold the needle with the cast-on stitches in your left hand. The first stitch on the left needle should be approximately one inch (2.5cm) from the tip of the needle. Hold the working needle in your right hand, wrapping the yarn around your fingers.

2 Insert the right needle from front to back into the first cast-on stitch on the left needle. Keep the right needle under the left needle and the yarn at the back.

3 Wrap the yarn under and over the right needle in a clockwise motion.

4 With the right needle, catch the yarn and pull it through the cast-on stitch.

5 Slip the cast-on stitch off the left needle, leaving the newly formed stitch on the right needle. Repeat these steps in each subsequent stitch until all stitches have been worked from the left needle. One knit row has been completed.

THE BASIC KNIT STITCH CONTINUED

(At one time, knitters used long double-pointed needles and wore a belted pouch around their waist, resting the right needle in a hole in the pouch.)

With the Continental method, you hold the yarn stationary in your left hand and use the right needle to pull the strand through to create a stitch. Although many consider this to be the quickest way to knit, the resulting fabric can sometimes be looser than fabric worked by the English method.

To learn the knit stitch, prepare by casting on a row of stitches. The directions on these pages show how to knit into each cast-on stitch, thus completing the first row (this row is always trickier to work since the tension has not yet been established). The yarn is always held to the back when knitting. After working the first row, switch the needle with the stitches to your opposite hand, and either work a second row of knit stitches to form garter stitch or go on to the purl stitch.

CONTINENTAL

1 Hold the needles in the same way as the English method on page 7, but wrap the yarn around your left hand rather than your right.

2 Insert the right needle from front to back into the first cast-on stitch on the left needle. Keep the right needle under the left needle, with the yarn in back of both needles.

3 Lay the yarn over the right needle as shown.

4 With the tip of the right needle, pull the strand through the cast-on stitch, holding the strand with the right index finger if necessary.

5 Slip the cast-on stitch off the left needle, leaving the newly formed stitch on the right needle. Continue to repeat these steps until you have worked all of the stitches from the left needle to the right needle. You have made one row of knit stitches.

THE BASIC PURL STITCH

You are ready to learn the second essential stitch—the purl stitch. The purl stitch is the reverse of the knit stitch. If you purl every row, your fabric will look the same as if you had knit every row. This is called garter stitch. If you alternate one row of purl stitches and one row of knit stitches, you create stockinette stitch, the most commonly used stitch. When you work stockinette stitch, the knit rows are the right side of the work and the purl rows are the wrong side. When you work the knit stitch and the purl stitch in the same row, you can create stitch patterns with dimension and texture.

ENGLISH

1 As with the knit stitch, hold the working needle in your right hand and the needle with the stitches in your left. The yarn is held and manipulated with your right hand and is kept to the front of the work.

2 Insert the right needle from back to front into the first stitch on the left needle. The right needle is now in front of the left needle and the yarn is at the front of the work.

3 With your right index finger, wrap the yarn counterclockwise around the right needle.

4 Draw the right needle and the yarn backward through the stitch on the left needle, forming a loop on the right needle.

5 Slip the stitch off the left needle. You have made one purl stitch. Repeat these steps in each subsequent stitch until all stitches have been worked from the left needle. One purl row has been completed.

THE BASIC PURL STITCH CONTINUED

When purling, the yarn and the needles are held in the same way as when knitting. The yarn, however, is kept to the front of the work rather than to the back, and the right needle is inserted into the stitch from back to front.

Working a purl stitch may be a bit more difficult for those who knit using the Continental method.

CONTINENTAL

1 As with the knit stitch, hold the working needle in your right hand and the needle with the stitches in your left. The yarn is held and manipulated with your left hand and is kept to the front of the work.

2 Insert the right needle from back to front into the first stitch on the left needle, keeping the yarn in front of the work.

3 Lay the yarn over the right needle as shown. Pull down on the yarn with your left index finger to keep the yarn taut.

4 Bring the right needle and the yarn backward through the stitch on the left needle, forming a loop on the right needle.

5 Slide the stitch off the left needle. Use your left index finger to tighten the new purl stitch on the right needle. Continue to repeat these steps until you have worked all of the stitches from the left needle to the right needle. You have made one row of purl stitches.

Basic Stitch Patterns

If you have knit or purled every row, you've made garter stitch. If you've worked alternate rows of knit and purl stitches, you've made stockinette stitch. If you turn the stockinette-stitch fabric around so that the purl stitches are on the right side of the work, you have reverse stockinettte stitch. These three stitches and the others shown here are simply different combinations of knit and purl stitches.

You will need to learn how to make ribbing before beginning your first garment. In ribbing, all the knit stitches line up over the knit stitches and all the purl stitches line up over the purl stitches. You must be able to recognize the difference between knit and purl stitches.

Once you have mastered basic rib stitches, try some twisted ribbings, which are made by working into the back loop of the stitch, which twists the stitch. In some twisted ribs, you work into the back loop of just the knit stitches; in others, you work into the back loops of both the knit and the purl stitches.

Seed stitch is a textured stitch created by working a sequence of knit and purl stitches, usually alternated on every row. Unlike ribbing, you knit the purl stitches and purl the knit stitches.

The instructions for these stitch patterns have been spelled out for beginners to understand.

Garter stitch

Any number of stitches
Knit every row.
Or
Purl every row.

Stockinette stitch

Any number of stitches
Row 1 (right side): Knit.
Row 2: Purl.
Repeat rows 1 and 2.

Reverse stockinette stitch

Any number of stitches
Row 1 (right side): Purl.
Row 2: Knit.
Repeat rows 1 and 2.

Garter ridge stitch

Any number of stitches
Rows 1 and 3 (right side): Knit.
Row 2: Purl.
Row 4: Knit.
Repeat rows 1 through 4.

Basic Stitch Patterns continued

Knit one, purl one ribbing

An odd number of stitches
Row 1 (right side): Knit one, *purl one, knit one; repeat from * to end.
Row 2: Purl one, *knit one, purl one; repeat from * to end.
Repeat rows 1 and 2.

Knit two, purl two ribbing

Multiple of 4 stitches plus 2 extra
Row 1 (right side): Knit two, *purl two, knit two; repeat from * to end.
Row 2: Purl two, *knit two, purl two; repeat from * to end.
Repeat rows 1 and 2.

Seed stitch

An even number of stitches
Row 1 (right side): *Knit one, purl one; repeat from * to end.
Row 2: Purl one, knit one; repeat from * to end.
Repeat rows 1 and 2.

Double seed stitch

An even number of stitches
Row 1 (right side): *Knit one, purl one; repeat from * to end.
Row 2: Repeat row 1.
Row 3: Purl one, knit one; repeat from * to end.
Row 4: Repeat row 3.
Repeat rows 1 through 4.

Twisted knit one, purl one ribbing (half twist)

An odd number of stitches
Row 1 (right side): Knit one through the back loop, *purl one, knit one through the back loop; repeat from * to end.
Row 2: Purl one, *knit one, purl one; repeat from * to end.
Repeat rows 1 and 2.

Twisted knit one, purl one ribbing (full twist)

An odd number of stitches
Row 1 (right side): Knit one through the back loop, *purl one, knit one through the back loop; repeat from * to end.
Row 2: Purl one through the back loop, *knit one, purl one through the back loop; repeat from * to end.
Repeat rows 1 and 2.

Knit Five, Purl Two Ribbing

Multiple of 7 stitches plus 5 extra
Row 1 (right side): Knit five, *purl two, knit five; repeat from * to end.
Row 2: Purl five, *knit two, purl five; repeat from * to end.
Repeat rows 1 and 2.

Knit Two, Purl Five Ribbing

Multiple of 7 stitches plus 2 extra
Row 1 (right side): Knit two, *purl five, knit two; repeat from * to end.
Row 2: Purl two, *knit five, purl two; repeat from * to end.
Repeat rows 1 and 2.

With yarn at back; with yarn at front

When knitting a stitch, the yarn is always held at the back of the work. When purling a stitch, the yarn is always at the front. In ribbing, when you change from a knit to a purl stitch, you must be sure the yarn is in the correct position to work the next stitch. When you are moving the yarn from the back to the front, or vice versa, the yarn should go between the two needles, and not over them.

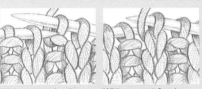

With yarn at back   With yarn at front

INCREASES

Increases are used to shape a piece of knitting by adding stitches to make it larger. Some increases are inconspicuous and do not interrupt the pattern, while others are visible and add a decorative touch. (Decorative increases are generally worked two or three stitches from the edge of the work.)

Most increases are worked on the right side of the work, for two reasons. First, you'll be able to see the finished look and placement of the increases. Also, it is easier to keep track of your increase rows when you work them at regular intervals, such as on every right-side row.

A knitting pattern may not specify the type of increase to be used. Increases that have a definite right or left slant can be placed to follow the slant of the increase. To choose an appropriate one, learn a variety of increases and note their characteristics. The symbolcraft symbol appears for each type of increase shown. Use these as a reference when working with patterns that are charted in symbolcraft.

If you want to add one or two stitches, use increases, but if you need to add several stitches at one time at the side edge, it is better to cast on the additional stitches.

BAR INCREASE—KNIT SIDE ☒ INC 1 ST

The bar increase is a visible increase. A horizontal bar will follow the increased stitch on the knit side of the work, whether you work the increase on the knit or the purl side.

1 To increase on the knit side, insert the right needle knitwise into the stitch to be increased. Wrap the yarn around the right needle and pull it through as if knitting, but leave the stitch on the left needle.

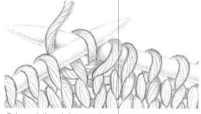

2 Insert the right needle into the back of the same stitch. Wrap the yarn around the needle and pull it through. Slip the stitch from the left needle. You now have two stitches on the right needle.

Working in front and back loops

The front of the stitch is the loop closest to you. Always work into the front loop unless otherwise stated. To knit into the front loop, insert the right needle from left to right into the stitch on the left needle. To knit into the back loop (loop farthest from you), insert right needle from right to left under left needle and into stitch. To purl into the front loop, insert needle from right to left into stitch. To purl into the back loop, insert needle from behind into stitch.

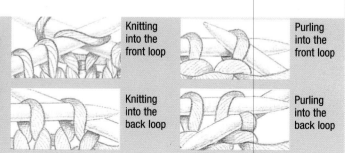

Knitting into the front loop

Purling into the front loop

Knitting into the back loop

Purling into the back loop

MAKE ONE: VERSION A  M1

The make one increase is made between two stitches and is practically invisible. This one slants to the right on the knit side.

1 Insert the left needle from back to front into the horizontal strand between the last stitch worked and the next stitch on the left needle.

2 Knit this strand through the front loop to twist the stitch.

To make the increase on the purl side, insert the left needle from back to front into the horizontal strand and purl it through the front loop.

MAKE ONE: VERSION B  M1

This make one method is similar to version A above, but it slants to the left on the knit side.

1 Insert the left needle from front to back into the horizontal strand between the last stitch worked and the first stitch on the left needle.

2 Knit this strand through the back loop to twist it.

To make the increase on the purl side, insert the left needle from front to back into the horizontal strand and purl it through the back loop.

MAKE ONE: VERSION C  M1

This decorative version of the make one increase creates a small hole because the stitch is not twisted.

On the knit side, insert the left needle from back to front into the horizontal strand between the two needles and knit it through the back loop.

On the purl side, insert the left needle from front to back into the horizontal strand between the two needles and purl it through the front loop.

Working multiple increases

When making multiple increases across a row, it is best to space them as evenly as possible. First, subtract one from the number of stitches to be increased. Divide this number into the number of stitches on the needle. For example, if there are 59 stitches on the needle and you need to increase nine stitches, then 9-1=8 and 59÷8=7 with a remainder of three. You would then have seven stitches between each increase with three remaining stitches to distribute over the ends.

If you are working the increase between the stitches, as in the make one increase, the instructions would be as follows: Work one stitch, [make one, work seven stitches] eight times, make one, work two stitches.

If you are using an increase that is worked into a stitch, such as the bar increase, then there are actually six stitches between each increase, as one of the seven stitches is being used for the increase. The instructions would be as follows: Work one stitch, [increase one stitch in the next stitch, work six stitches] eight times, increase one stitch in the next stitch, work one stitch.

DECREASES

Decreasing is a method of reducing the number of stitches (usually one or two at a time) to narrow a piece of knitting.

As with increases, a variety of methods can be used, depending on the purpose they will serve. For example, decreases can slant to the left, slant to the right, or be vertical. When shaping an armhole, you might want to work a left-slanting decrease on the right-hand side of the garment, and a right-slanting decrease on the left-hand side of the garment, thus emphasizing the slope of the shaping. If placed one or two stitches in from the edge, the decreases become a decorative detail. This type of visible decreasing is called "full-fashioned" decreasing. Placing the decreases away from the edge also makes it easier to seam the pieces together.

Of course, the decreases do not have to be visible. A simple decrease (such as knitting two stitches together) can be placed at the edge of the knitting so that it will be invisible once the pieces are sewn together.

Most decreases are worked on the right side of the knitting, but sometimes it is necessary to decrease stitches on the wrong side (such as when the decreases are worked on every row). For this reason, we have included in this chapter decreases that can be worked on the purl side of the work.

Basic single left-slanting decrease  k2tog tbl

Knitting (or purling) two stitches together through the back loops is a decrease that slants the stitches to the left on the knit side of the work. It is abbreviated as k2tog tbl (or p2tog tbl).

With the right needle behind the left needle, insert the right needle through the back loops of the next two stitches on the left needle. Knit these two stitches together.

With the right needle behind the left needle, insert the right needle into the back loop of the second stitch, and then into the back loop of the first stitch on the left needle, which twists the two stitches. Purl these two stitches together.

Basic single right-slanting decrease  k2tog

Knitting (or purling) two stitches together is the easiest technique and one that every beginner must learn. This basic decrease slants to the right on the knit side of the work. It is abbreviated as k2tog (or p2tog).

Insert the right needle from front to back (knitwise) into the next two stitches on the left needle. Wrap the yarn around the right needle (as when knitting) and pull it through. You have decreased one stitch.

Insert the right needle into the front loops (purlwise) of the next two stitches on the left needle. Wrap the yarn around the right needle (as when purling) and pull it through. You have decreased one stitch.

SINGLE LEFT-SLANTING DECREASE: VERSION A ⊠ SKP

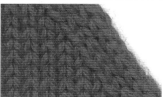

This decrease slants the stitches to the left on the knit side of the work. It is abbreviated as SKP or sl 1, k1, psso (slip one stitch, knit one stitch, pass slip stitch over knit stitch).

1 Slip one stitch knitwise, then knit the next stitch. Insert the left needle into the slipped stitch as shown.

2 Pass the slipped stitch over the knit stitch and off the right needle.

SINGLE LEFT-SLANTING DECREASE: VERSION B ⊠ SSK

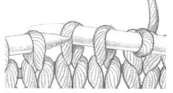

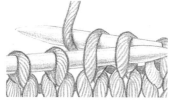

This decrease slants the stitches to the left on the knit side of the work. It is abbreviated as ssk (slip one, slip one, knit two together).

1 Slip two stitches knitwise, one at a time, from the left needle to the right needle.

2 Insert the left needle into the fronts of these two slipped stitches as shown and knit them together.

SINGLE LEFT-SLANTING DECREASE: VERSION C ⊠

This decrease, worked on the purl side, slants the stitches to the left on the knit side.

1 Slip two stitches knitwise, one at a time, from the left needle to the right needle. Return these two slipped stitches to the left needle as shown, keeping them twisted.

2 Purl these two stitches together through the back loops.

SINGLE RIGHT-SLANTING DECREASE: VERSION A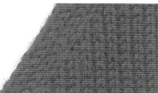

This decrease slants stitches to the right on the knit side.

1 Knit one stitch, slip one stitch knitwise; return the slipped stitch (keeping it twisted) and the knit stitch (as shown) to the left needle.

2 Pass the slipped stitch over the knit stitch and off the left needle as shown. Slip the knit stitch purlwise to the right needle.

SINGLE RIGHT-SLANTING DECREASE: VERSION B

This decrease, worked on the purl side, slants stitches to the right on the knit side.

1 Slip the next stitch on the left needle purlwise, then purl one stitch as shown.

2 With the left needle, pass the slipped stitch over the purl stitch and off the right needle.

DOUBLE LEFT-SLANTING DECREASE: VERSION A

This method decreases two stitches and slants to the left on the knit side.

1 Slip the next stitch knitwise, then knit the next two stitches together as shown to decrease one stitch.

2 Pass the slipped stitch over the decreased stitch.

Double left-slanting decrease: version B

This method, worked on the purl side, decreases two stitches and slants to the left on the knit side.

1 Purl two stitches together and return this decreased stitch to the left needle as shown.

2 Pass the second stitch on the left needle over the decreased stitch and off the needle. Then return the decreased stitch to the right needle.

Double right-slanting decrease: version A

This method decreases two stitches and slants to the right on the knit side.

1 Slip one stitch knitwise, knit the next stitch, pass the slipped stitch over the knit stitch (SKP). Return this decreased stitch to the left needle.

2 Pass the second stitch on the left needle over the decreased stitch and off the needle. Return the decreased stitch to the right needle.

Double right-slanting decrease: version B

This method, worked on the purl side, decreases two stitches and slants to the right on the knit side.

1 Slip one stitch purlwise, then purl two stitches together as shown.

2 Pass the slipped stitch over the decreased stitch.

Double vertical decrease: version A

This method decreases two stitches and creates a vertical stitch.

1 Insert the right needle into the next two stitches on the left needle as if you were knitting them together and slip them to the right needle.

2 Knit the next stitch on the left needle. With the left needle, pull both slipped stitches over the knit stitch as shown.

Double vertical decrease: version B

1 Working from the purl side, insert the right needle into the next two stitches on the left needle one at a time as if you were knitting them. Slip them to the right needle. You now have two twisted stitches on the right needle.

2 Return the two slipped stitches to the left needle, keeping them twisted.

3 Insert the right needle through the back loops of the second and the first slipped stitches and slip them together off the left needle.

4 Purl the next stitch. With the left needle, pass the two slipped stitches over the purl stitch and off the right needle.

Slipping a stitch knitwise and purlwise

To slip a stitch is to pass it from one needle to another without working it. It is sometimes done when decreasing as well as when working color and stitch patterns. A stitch slipped purlwise remains untwisted, but slipped knitwise, it will twist. If instructions do not specify which way to slip the stitch, slip it purlwise except when decreasing; in this case, slip knit stitches knitwise and purl stitches purlwise.

To slip one stitch purlwise, insert the right needle into the next stitch on the left needle as if you were purling the stitch. Pull this stitch off the left needle. The stitch is now on the right needle.

To slip one stitch knitwise, insert the right needle into the next stitch on the left needle as if you were knitting the stitch. Pull this stitch off the left needle. The stitch is now on the right needle and twisted.

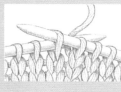

Slip one stitch purlwise

Slip one stitch knitwise

BINDING OFF

Binding off links stitches that are no longer to be worked and keeps them from unraveling. The resulting selvage can be connected to other pieces of knitting or it can stand on its own. The bound-off edge should be elastic, but firm—not too loose or too tight. Knitters often tend to bind off too tightly. A way to reduce this tendency is to use a larger needle to bind off. Unless otherwise stated, you should bind off in the stitch pattern used for the piece.

Binding off is not only used for finishing knit pieces, but also for shaping armholes, necks, and shoulders. It can be the first row of a buttonhole, or it can be used to create three-dimensional stitch patterns.

If you bind off all the stitches in the row, pull the yarn through the last stitch to fasten off the piece.

Basic knit bind-off

This is the most common bind-off method and the easiest to learn. It creates a firm, neat edge.

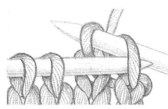

1 Knit two stitches. *Insert the left needle into the first stitch on the right needle.

2 Pull this stitch over the second stitch and off the right needle.

3 One stitch remains on the right needle as shown. Knit the next stitch. Repeat from the * until you have bound off the required number of stitches.

Basic purl bind-off

The purl bind-off creates a firm edge and is used on purl stitches.

1 Purl two stitches. *Insert the left needle from behind the right needle into the back loop of the first stitch on the right needle as shown.

2 Pull this stitch over the second stitch and off the right needle.

3 One stitch remains on the right needle as shown. Purl the next stitch. Repeat from the * until you have bound off the required number of stitches.

THREE-NEEDLE BIND-OFF

This bind-off is used to join two edges that have the same number of stitches, such as shoulder edges, which have been placed on holders.

1 With the right side of the two pieces facing each other, and the needles parallel, insert a third needle knitwise into the first stitch of each needle. Wrap the yarn around the needle as if to knit.

2 Knit these two stitches together and slip them off the needles. *Knit the next two stitches together in the same way as shown.

3 Slip the first stitch on the third needle over the second stitch and off the needle. Repeat from the * in step 2 across the row until all the stitches are bound off.

II. Understanding Knitting Instructions

GAUGE

Gauge is the number of stitches and rows per inch, based on the size of a knitted stitch. The size of a stitch depends on the yarn, the needle size, and how you control the yarn.

Controlling the yarn through your fingers is similar to setting the tension dial on a sewing or knitting machine to determine how tightly the thread feeds through the needle. Each knitter has a different way of controlling the yarn, which can further vary depending on the type of yarn and needles used (or even the knitter's mood). Since no two knitters work alike, one knitter may have to use a different needle size than another to obtain the same gauge.

Another factor that affects gauge is yarn substitution. A different yarn can alter the gauge as well as produce a different texture. Gauges using the same quality yarns may differ from color to color. For example, a black yarn can have a different gauge than the same type of yarn in white.

Even the type of needle that you use can affect the gauge. You may obtain a slightly different gauge using aluminum needles than you would with plastic or wooden ones.

Make sure that you use the same type of yarn, color, and needles throughout your project.

If you do not achieve the exact gauge, you will alter the size as well as the texture of your finished garment. That is why it is imperative to check your gauge before beginning every project.

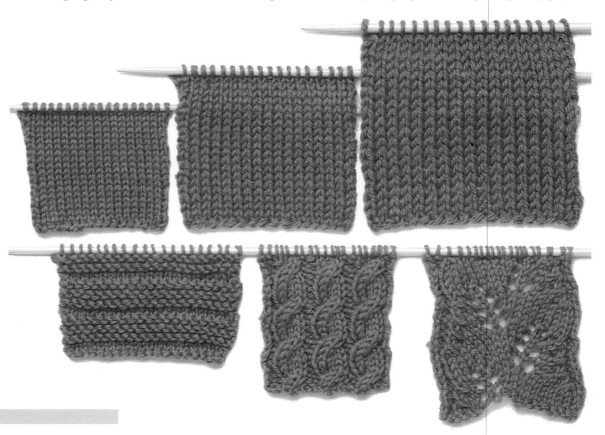

Each swatch was made in stockinette stitch with the same number of stitches and rows, but using three different needle sizes, from smaller to larger. The smaller the needle, the smaller the swatch, and the larger the needle, the larger the swatch.

Here are three different pattern stitches that were made using the same needle size and the same number of stitches and rows, but resulting in three different finished sizes.

How to make a gauge swatch

A gauge swatch is a small piece of knitting, made before beginning a garment, that is used to make sure you can obtain the gauge given in the instructions.

Normally the gauge is given for four inches (10cm) square. Your swatch should be at least this size to make measuring easier and to give a more accurate gauge. If the gauge is given for a smaller piece, you will have to calculate the stitches and rows needed to make four inches (10cm). For example, if the gauge is given for one inch, multiply the number of stitches and rows by four; if given for two inches, multiply by two.

Using the needles and yarn suggested, cast on the number of stitches required to get at least four inches (10cm). You may also add two garter stitches at each edge to make it easier to measure between them. (If so, be sure to add these extra stitches when you cast on for your swatch.) Or make a swatch that is four to six stitches and rows larger than the stated gauge and measure the correct number of stitches between pins you place in the work.

Frequently, the gauge is given in stockinette stitch. However, if the gauge calls for a specific pattern stitch, work this stitch for your swatch. It may not always be possible to obtain a four-inch (10cm) square when working in a stitch pattern because the swatch has to be a specific number of stitches. To determine your gauge, you can either use the center four inches (10cm) or measure the entire swatch and divide that measurement by the number of stitches to get the number of stitches per inch.

If you are knitting several different stitch patterns in one garment, such as an Aran sweater, and the instructions give one gauge for all the patterns, make one large swatch, incorporating all the stitch patterns.

When working with lacy patterns or yarns that stretch, such as cottons or silks, make your swatch at least six to eight inches (15cm to 20cm) square so that both horizontal and vertical stretch are taken into account. Block the swatch before measuring it.

If no pattern is given, you can assume that the gauge is in stockinette stitch.

Instead of binding off the last row of your swatch, place it on a stitch holder or simply cut the yarn and thread it through the stitches before you remove them from the needle. Binding off may pull in the stitches at the top and make measuring your swatch more difficult. However, if it is a lacy pattern or one that tends to spread, you should bind off the last row.

If your gauge matches the one given, you can proceed with your knitting. But if it does not match exactly, you must try another swatch until you can achieve the correct gauge. If your swatch is smaller than the stated gauge, try larger needles. If it is larger, use smaller needles. Label each swatch with the needle size, number of stitches, and gauge for future reference.

With some yarns, such as mohairs and bouclés, the stitches are difficult to count individually because they are less defined. You should therefore cast on the exact number of stitches given in the gauge, work the specified number of rows, and measure the entire swatch. Or place stitch markers on either side of the stitches needed for the gauge, and measure between the markers.

You must use a different technique to make a gauge swatch for a garment that is knit in the round, especially if it is stockinette stitch. When you work stockinette in the round, you knit every row, never purling. Since knitting differs slightly from purling, the gauge for straight knitting will differ from that for circular knitting. It is possible to make a swatch without working in the round by knitting every row on a circular or two double-pointed needles as follows: After the first row, cut the yarn. Slide the stitches to the other end of the needle to begin a new row, without turning your work. Repeat at the end of each row.

How to check and measure gauge

It is easiest to measure stitches on a flat, even swatch. You may need to steam or wet block your swatch after taking it off the needles, unless the finishing instructions say not to block. Pin the swatch on a flat surface, such as an ironing board, and do not stretch it.

When the swatch is thoroughly dry, measure the gauge with a tape measure or stitch gauge. Be sure to count the stitches carefully because a variation of even half a stitch will make a significant difference in your finished piece.

With certain fabrics, such as ribs, you may have to stretch the fabric slightly to obtain an accurate gauge.

Your gauge may change from your swatch to your knitted piece because your style of knitting may be different when you have only a few stitches on the needle. Check your knitting after working five or six inches (12cm or 15cm) to be sure the gauge is accurate. If it has changed, you will have to knit the piece again using the next size needle, measuring again after several inches.

Importance of row gauge

Some knitters believe that the row gauge is not as essential as the stitch gauge. This is not necessarily true. In shaping pieces, such as sleeves, if you work the increases given in the instructions without getting the proper row gauge, you may alter the length. When you work a sweater from a full body chart, you must work the exact number of rows on the chart. If you do not have the correct row gauge, your finished piece will be too long or too short.

Some sweaters are worked from side to side. In this case, the rows determine the width, making the row gauge essential for proper fit.

Uses for gauge swatches

Not only do gauge swatches help ensure the success of your projects, they can have many other useful purposes:
- Use them to practice borders, buttonholes, embroidery, and finishes.
- Sew squares together to make an afghan or blanket.
- Put swatches in a notebook to keep for future reference.
- Test the yarn's washability or colorfastness.

Measuring gauge

You can measure your gauge swatch between selvage stitches using a tape measure, as the first two photos show. Or you can use a stitch gauge in the center of your swatch and count the stitches and rows inside the two-inch (5cm) right angle opening, as shown in the third photo.

ABBREVIATIONS EXPLAINED

A

alt—alternate; alternately

Alternate increases or decreases are used when shaping pieces to create an even slant. For example, in the illustration above, the increases or decreases (highlighted in yellow) are worked alternately every fourth and sixth rows. This means the first increase or decrease is worked on the fourth row. Five rows are worked even, and then the stitches are increased or decreased again on the next row (the sixth row after the first increase or decrease, or the tenth row from the beginning). Therefore, every ten rows you work two sets of increases or decreases.

approx—approximately

B

BC—back cross; back cable (see cable)

beg—begin; begins; beginning

BO—bind off

BO—bobble (see MB)

C

C—cable; cross   A cable (also called cross) is formed by using an extra needle, usually a cable needle or double-pointed needle, to hold stitches to be crossed either to the front (which crosses them to the left), or to the back (which crosses them to the right). The cable crossing is worked on the right side of the work. The extra needle should be thinner than those you are working with to avoid stretching the stitches. After you have worked the cable, be sure to pull the yarn firmly before working the next stitch to prevent gaps in your work. The illustrations below show examples of a six-stitch front (or left) cable and a six-stitch back (or right) cable.

Front (or left) cable

Back (or right) cable

FRONT (OR LEFT) CABLE

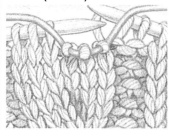

1 Slip the first three stitches of the cable purlwise to a cable needle and hold them to the front of the work. Be careful not to twist the stitches.

2 Leave the stitches suspended in front of the work, keeping them in the center of the cable needle where they won't slip off. Pull the yarn firmly and knit the next three stitches.

3 Knit the three stitches from the cable needle. If this seems too awkward, return the stitches to the left needle and then knit them.

BACK (OR RIGHT) CABLE

1 Slip the first three stitches of the cable purlwise to a cable needle and hold them to the back of the work. Be careful not to twist the stitches.

2 Leave the stitches suspended in back of the work, keeping them in the center of the cable needle where they won't slip off. Pull the yarn firmly and knit the next three stitches.

3 Knit the three stitches from the cable needle. If this seems too awkward, return the stitches to the left needle and then knit them.

CC—contrasting color When two colors are used, the contrasting color is the yarn that is used as an accent.

ch—chain

cm—centimeter(s)

cn—cable needle

CO—cast on

cont—continue; continuing

cross 2 L—cross two stitches to the left (see cable)

cross 2 R—cross two stitches to the right (see cable)

D

dc—double crochet

dec—decrease; decreasing

decs—decreases

DK—double knitting

dp; dpn—double-pointed needle

dtr—double treble

E

EON—end of needle

F

FC—front cross (see cable)

foll—follow; follows; following

G

g; gr—gram

grp; grps—group; groups

g st—garter stitch

H

hdc—half double crochet

hk—hook

I

in; ins—inch; inches

inc—increase; increasing

incl—including

incs—increases

K

k—knit

k-b; k1-b—knit stitch in row below (infrequently used for knit through back loop—see tbl)

With the yarn at the back, insert the right needle from front to back into the center of the stitch one row below the next stitch on the left needle. Knit this stitch. Slip the top stitch off the left needle without working it.

kfb—knit into the front and back of a stitch

k tbl—knit through back loop

k2tog—knit two together

kwise—knitwise

L

LC—left cross (see cable)

LH—left-hand

lp; lps—loop; loops

LT—left twist A left twist is formed by crossing one stitch over another. Work this as a two-stitch cable using a cable needle, or use any of the following three methods. All slant to the left.

From the knit side: Version A

1 Skip the first stitch on the left needle. With the right needle behind the left one, insert the right needle into the back loop of the second stitch on the left needle. Wrap the yarn knitwise and pull it through.

2 Knit the skipped stitch through the front loop as shown and slip both stitches from the left needle.

From the knit side: Version B

Knit the second stitch through the back loop as for version A. Then knit the first and second stitches together through the back loops.

From the purl side

1 Skip the first stitch on the left needle and purl the second stitch through the back loop as shown.

2 Purl the skipped stitch through the front loop as shown and slip both stitches from the left needle.

M

m—meter(s)

MB—make bobble   A bobble is a three-dimensional stitch made by working multiple increases in one stitch, sometimes working a few rows, and then decreasing back to one stitch. The following example is of a five-stitch bobble.

Make bobble

1 Make five stitches in one stitch as follows: [knit the stitch in the front loop and then knit in the back loop without slipping it from the left needle] twice, knit in the front loop once more. Slip the stitch from the left needle.

2 [Turn the work and purl these five stitches as shown, turn the work and knit five] twice.

3 With the left needle, pull the second, third, fourth, and fifth stitches one at a time over the first stitch and off the needle. One bobble has been made.

MC—main color   When two or more colors are used, the main color is the yarn that is dominant.

mm—millimeter(s)

m1—make one

N

no—number

O

oz—ounce

P

p—purl

pat; pats—pattern; patterns

p-b; p 1 b—purl stitch in row below

With the yarn at the front, insert the right needle from back to front into the center of the stitch one row below the stitch on the left needle. Purl this stitch. Slip the top stitch off the left needle without working it.

pfb—purl into the front and back of a stitch

pnso—pass next stitch over

psso—pass slip stitch over

p tbl—purl through back loop

p2tog—purl two together

pwise—purlwise

R

RC—right cross (see cable)

rem—remain; remaining

rep—repeat

rev St st—reverse stockinette stitch

RH—right-hand

rib—ribbing

rnd; rnds—round; rounds

RS—right side

RT—right twist   A right twist is formed by crossing one stitch over another. Work this as a two-stitch cable using a cable needle, or use any of the following three methods. All slant to the right.

FROM THE KNIT SIDE: VERSION A

1 Knit two stitches together through front loops. Do not slip them from the left needle.

2 Then knit the first stitch through the front loop as shown. Slip both stitches from the left needle.

FROM THE KNIT SIDE: VERSION B

Skip the first stitch on the left needle. Insert the right needle into the front loop of the second stitch on the left needle. Wrap yarn knitwise and pull it through; do not slip the stitch off the needle. Knit the skipped stitch through the front loop and slip both stitches from the left needle.

FROM THE PURL SIDE

1 Skip the first stitch on the left needle and purl the second stitch through the front loop as shown.

2 Purl the skipped stitch through the front loop as shown and slip both stitches from the left needle.

S

sc—single crochet

sk—skip

SKP—slip one, knit one, pass slip stitch over

sl—slip

sl st—slip stitch

sp; sps—space; spaces

ssk—slip, slip, knit

st; sts—stitch; stitches

St st—stockinette stitch

T

tbl—through back loop

tch; t-ch—turning chain

tog—together

tr—treble

trtr—triple treble

W

WS—wrong side

won—wool over needle

wrn—wool round needle

wyib—with yarn in back

wyif—with yarn in front

Y

yb (or ybk)—yarn to the back

yf (or yfwd)—yarn to the front (or forward)

yfon—yarn forward and over needle (see yarn over)

yfrn—yarn forward and round needle (see yarn over)

yo—yarn over   A yarn over is a decorative increase made by wrapping the yarn around the needle. There are various ways to make a yarn over depending on where it is placed.

yo twice; yo2—yarn over two times

yon—yarn over needle (see yarn over)

yrn—yarn round needle (see yarn over)

Yarn overs

Between two knit stitches

Bring the yarn from the back of the work to the front between the two needles. Knit the next stitch, bringing the yarn to the back over the right needle as shown.

Between a knit and a purl stitch

Bring the yarn from the back to the front between the two needles, then to the back over the right needle and to the front again as shown. Purl the next stitch.

Between a purl and a knit stitch

Leave the yarn at the front of the work. Knit the next stitch, bringing the yarn to the back over the right needle as shown.

Between two purl stitches

Leave the yarn at the front of the work. Bring the yarn to the back over the right needle and to the front again as shown. Purl the next stitch.

At the beginning of a knit row

Keep the yarn at the front of the work. Insert the right needle knitwise into the first stitch on the left needle. Bring the yarn over the right needle to the back and knit the next stitch, holding the yarn over with your thumb if necessary.

At the beginning of a purl row

To work a yarn over at the beginning of a purl row, keep the yarn at the back of the work. Insert the right needle purlwise into the first stitch on the left needle. Purl the stitch.

Multiple yarn overs

1 For multiple yarn overs (two or more), wrap the yarn around the needle as for a single yarn over, then wrap the yarn around the needle once more (or as many times as indicated). Work the next stitch on the left needle.

2 Alternate knitting and purling into the multiple yarn over on the subsequent row, always knitting the last stitch on a purl row and purling the last stitch on a knit row.

KNITTING TERMINOLOGY

A

above markers: Knitting worked after the point where stitch markers have been placed.

above rib: Knitting worked after the last row of ribbing.

after . . . number of rows have been worked: Continue working as instructed after completing the designated number of rows.

along neck: Generally used when picking up stitches at an unshaped, or straight, neck edge.

around neck: Generally used when picking up stitches at a shaped, or curved, neck edge.

as established: Continue to work the pattern as previously described.

as foll: Work the instructions that follow.

as for back (front): Work a piece identical to the back (or the front).

as to knit: Work the stitch as if you were knitting.

as to purl: Work the stitch as if you were purling.

AT SAME TIME: Work the instructions that immediately follow this term simultaneously with those that immediately precede it.

attach: Join a new strand of yarn.

B

back edge: Any edge on the back piece of the garment.

beg and end as indicated: Used when working with charts. Begin the row of knitting at the point on the chart that is indicated for your size by an arrow or straight line and the term "beg" (beginning). Continue working the chart as instructed, knitting the last stitch at the point indicated by another arrow or straight line and the term "end."

bind off . . . sts at beg of next . . . rows: Often used in armhole and shoulder shaping. Stitches are almost always bound off at the beginning of a row. Therefore, after binding off the designated number of stitches, work to the end of the row, turn the work, and bind off the same number of stitches at the beginning of the next row.

bind off center . . . sts: Determine the center stitches and place markers on either side of the center stitches, if desired, on the needles. Work the next row to the first marker, join a new ball of yarn and bind off the center stitches, then work to the end of the row with the new ball of yarn.

bind off from each neck edge: A term used when both sides of the inside neck edge are shaped simultaneously after binding off the center stitches.

bind off in rib (or pat): Always bind off stitches as they appear. That is, knit the knit stitches and purl the purl stitches as you bind them off.

bind off loosely: Do not pull the yarn too tightly when binding off. Or, you may use a needle one size larger on the bind-off row.

bind off rem sts each side: A term usually used for the remaining stitches of each shoulder after shaping a neck. After you have completed all the shaping, bind off the stitches that remain on one side, then bind off the remaining stitches on the other side.

block pieces: The process of laying flat completed pieces of knitting to even and smooth the stitches and to give them their permanent shape.

body of sweater is worked in one piece to underarm: A term used when using a circular needle to knit a sweater with no side seams up to the underarm.

both sides at once (or at same time): A term used after an opening has been made on a row, such as for a placket. When stitches have been bound off and you have two separate pieces on one needle, work both sides simultaneously with separate balls of yarn. That is, work one row on the first side, then work the corresponding row on the second side with the second ball of yarn. Then turn the work.

C

cap shaping: The shaped part of the sleeve above the widest part of the arm, which will fit into the armhole of the sweater.

carry yarn loosely across back of work: In color knitting, let the yarn not in use span loosely across the wrong side of the work until you need to use it again.

cast on . . . sts at beg of next . . . rows: When adding two or more stitches at the edges of a piece, cast on the designated number of stitches before beginning the row, work the cast-on stitches, then work to the end of the row. Turn the work and cast on the same number of stitches at the beginning of the next row.

cast on . . . sts over bound-off sts: Usually refers to making buttonholes. Work to where the stitches from the previous row were bound off. Cast on the specified number of stitches, then work to the end of the row.

center back (front) neck: The point that marks the center of the back (or front) neck.

change to smaller (larger) needles: Proceed with the work using smaller (or larger) needles than those used previously.

cont in pat: Continue to work the pattern as previously described.

cont in this way: Continue to work in the manner previously described.

D

directions are for smallest (smaller) size with larger sizes in parentheses: Many knitting instructions are written for more than one size. Usually, the number referring to the smallest (smaller) size is the number before the parentheses. The numbers indicating larger sizes appear inside the parentheses in ascending order.

discontinue pat: Stop working the pattern immediately preceding and continue as directed.

do not press: Do not use an iron to press or steam the knitted fabric.

do not turn work: Keep the work facing in the same direction as the row you have just completed.

E

each end (side): Work designated stitches at both the beginning and the end of a row.

easing in any fullness: In seaming, gather in any extra fabric evenly.

end last rep: After completing a full repeat of a pattern and not enough stitches remain to complete another

repeat, end the pattern repeat as directed.

end with a RS (WS) row: The last row worked is a right side (wrong side) row.

every other row: When shaping, work one row between each increase or decrease row.

F

fasten off: When binding off, pull the yarn through the last loop on the needle to finish the piece and prevent unraveling.

finished bust: The circumference of a garment at the bustline after the front and back have been sewn together.

finished bust (buttoned): A term usually used for cardigans or jackets to indicate the circumference at the bustline after the two fronts and the back have been sewn together and the fronts are buttoned.

from beg: A term used when measuring from the cast-on edge of the piece or beginning of the knitted piece.

front edge: Any edge on the front piece of the garment.

full-fashioned: A term used in ready-to-wear that means deliberately showing decreases or increases worked in stockinette stitch a few stitches from the edge.

G

gauge: The number of stitches and rows per inch (centimeter).

grafting: Weaving two edges together that have not been bound off, resulting in an invisible joining.

H

hold to front (back) of work: A term usually referring to stitches placed on a cable needle that are held to the front (or the back) of the work as it faces you.

I

inc . . . sts evenly across row: Increase the stitches at even intervals across the row.

inc sts into pat: When increasing, work the added stitches into the established pattern.

in same way (manner): Repeat the process that was previously described.

it is essential to get proper row gauge: When instructions are written for a specific number of rows (such as in garments with large motifs), you must obtain the specified row gauge to get the correct length.

J

join: When used in circular knitting, the process of uniting the first and last stitch of a round.

join 2nd ball (skein) of yarn: A phrase used when dividing the work into two sections (such as for placket or neck shaping), where each section is worked with a separate ball (or skein) of yarn.

join, taking care not to twist sts: When casting on in circular knitting, join the first and the last cast-on stitch to form a circle, making sure that the stitches are not twisted on the needle.

K

k the knit sts and p the purl sts (as they face you): A phrase used when a pattern of knit and purl stitches has been established and will continue for a determined length (such as ribbing). Work the stitches as they face you: Knit the knit stitches and purl the purl stitches.

k the purl sts and p the knit sts: A phrase used when a pattern of knit and purl stitches will alternate on the following row or rows (such as in a seed stitch pattern). Work the stitches opposite of how they face you: Purl the knit stitches and knit the purl stitches.

keep careful count of rows: Advice usually given with intricate patterns or shaping in which the row count is important. Keep track either by writing down each row as you complete it or by using a row counter.

keeping to pat (or maintaining pat): A term used when new instructions are given (such as shaping), but the established pattern must be continued.

knitwise (or as to knit): Insert the needle into the stitch as if you were going to knit it.

L

left: Refers to the left-hand side of the garment as you are wearing it.

lower edge: The bottom edge of the piece, usually the cast-on edge.

M

matching colors: Work the stitches in the same color sequence as on the previous row.

multiple of . . . sts: Used when working a pattern. The total number of stitches should be divisible by the number of stitches in one pattern repeat.

multiple of . . . sts plus . . . extra: Used when working a pattern. The total number of stitches should be divisible by the number of stitches in one pattern repeat, plus the extra stitches (added only once).

N

next row (RS), or (WS): The row following the one just worked will be a right side (or wrong side) row.

O

on all foll rows: A direction that applies to all the rows that follow the row just worked.

P

pick up and k: Used in finishing to refer to pulling up loops through stitches and rows of a finished edge with the stated knitting needles and a ball of yarn to begin an edge or a new piece.

piece measures approx: A term used when a specified number of rows must be worked, as in shaping or pattern work. The piece should measure the stated amount within one-fourth inch (6mm) if you have the correct row gauge.

place marker(s): Slide a stitch marker either onto the needle (where it is slipped every row) or attach it to a stitch, where it remains as a guide.

preparation row: A row that sets up the stitch pattern but is not part of the pattern repeat.

pull up a lp: Often used in crochet, this term in knitting signifies drawing a new stitch (or loop) through the knit fabric.

purlwise: Insert the needle into the stitch as if you were going to purl it.

R

rep between *'s: Repeat the instructions that fall between the two asterisks.

rep from * around: In circular knitting, repeat the instructions that begin at the asterisk, ending at the joining.

rep from *, end . . . : Repeat the instructions that begin at the asterisk as many times as you can work full repeats of the pattern, then end the row as directed.

rep from * to end: Repeat the instructions that begin at the asterisk, ending the row with a full repeat of the pattern.

rep from . . . row: Repeat the pattern rows previously worked, beginning with the row specified.

rep inc (or dec): Repeat the increase (or decrease) previously described.

rep . . . times more: Repeat a direction the designated number of times (not counting the first time you work it).

reverse pat placement: A term used for garments such as cardigans where the right and left fronts have symmetrical patterns. Generally, the instructions for only one piece are given, and you must work patterns for the second piece in the opposite order.

reversing shaping: A term used for garments such as cardigans where shaping for the right and left fronts is identical, but reversed. The instructions for only one piece are given, and you must work the shaping for the second piece in the opposite order.

right: Refers to the right-hand side of the garment as you are wearing it.

right side (or RS): Usually refers to the surface of the work that will face outside when the garment is worn.

row: A horizontal line of stitches formed by transferring all the stitches from one needle to the other.

row 2 and all WS (even-numbered) rows: A term used when all the wrong-side or even-numbered rows are worked the same.

S

same as: Follow the instructions given in another section or piece of the garment.

same length as: A term used when two or more pieces of a garment are equal in length, and the measurement of one has already been given.

schematic: A scale drawing showing specific measurements of all the pieces of a garment before they are sewn together and finished.

selvage st: An extra stitch (or stitches) at the edge of a piece used either to make seaming easier or as a decorative finish.

set in sleeves: Sew the sleeves into the armholes.

S CONTINUED

sew shoulder seam, including neckband: A phrase used when seaming a shoulder before working a neckband. After the neckband is completed, sew the open shoulder seam along with the side edges of the neckband.

sew top of sleeves between markers: A term generally used when the garment has no armhole shaping (such as for drop shoulders), and markers must be used to denote the depth of the armhole. Center the sleeve at the shoulder seam, with the ends of the sleeve top at the markers, and sew it to the front and back of the garment.

short row: A technique, generally used in shaping, to add rows in one segment of a piece without decreasing the number of stitches on the needle.

side to side: When a piece is worked horizontally from side seam to side seam instead of vertically from the lower edge.

sleeve width at upper arm: The measurement of the finished sleeve at its widest point, which, when seamed, fits around the widest part of the arm.

slightly stretched: A term often used when measuring stitch patterns that tend to pull in, such as ribbing or cables. A more accurate gauge of the pattern is obtained when the stitches are pulled apart slightly.

slip marker: To keep the stitch marker in the same position from one row to the next, transfer it from one needle to the other as you work each row.

slip marker at beg of every rnd: In circular knitting, slip the marker from one needle to the other every time you begin a new round.

slip sts to a holder: Transfer the stitches from the needle to a stitch holder.

swatch: A sample of knitting used to check the gauge or to try out a stitch or colorwork pattern before knitting the garment.

sweater is worked in one piece: Work all the parts of a sweater—the front, back, and sleeves—as one piece.

sweater is worked in two pieces: Work the front half of the sweater (including the front half of the sleeves) in one piece and the back half in another.

T

through both thicknesses: A term usually used in seaming when working through two pieces of fabric at one time.

through . . . row: Work up to and include the designated row. This term is usually used when knitting from a chart.

to . . . row: Work up to but do not include the specified row. This term is usually used when knitting from a chart.

total length: The length of a garment after finishing, including ribbing or edging and any shoulder shaping.

turning: The process of switching your knitted piece from right side to wrong side or vice versa to work a new or partial row.

turning ridge: A row of raised stitches (often purl stitches on stockinette stitch) that indicates where the piece will fold in or out, as in a hem.

twist yarns on WS to prevent holes: A term used in colorwork when changing from one color to the next across a row. Twist the old and the new yarns around each other to prevent a hole in your work.

U

use a separate bobbin for each block of color: When working intarsia (large color block patterns), where the yarn cannot be carried across large areas of color, use a bobbin for each separate block of color.

W

weave in ends: In finishing, loose ends must be worked in so that they will not unravel.

when armhole measures: This term is used to denote the point in a sweater at which the neck, shoulder, or placket shaping begins and is measured from the beginning of the armhole shaping.

weave or twist yarns not in use: In Fair Isle knitting, when you must carry yarns for more than a few stitches, weave or twist yarns that are not being used around the working yarn to avoid long, loose strands.

width from sleeve edge (cuff) to sleeve edge (cuff): When the body and sleeves of a sweater are knit in one piece, this term refers to the width measurement from the edge of one sleeve, across the shoulder and neck edges, to the edge of the second sleeve.

with RS facing: A term often used when picking up stitches. The right side of the work must be facing you and the wrong side facing away from you.

with WS facing: A term used when the wrong side of the work must be facing you and the right side facing away from you.

work across sts on holder: Work the stitches directly from the stitch holder, or transfer the stitches from the holder to a knitting needle and then work them.

work back and forth as with straight needles: When knitting on a circular needle, turn the work at the end of every row instead of joining it and working in rounds.

work buttonholes opposite markers: When markers for buttons have been placed on the button band, work the buttonholes opposite these markers on the other band so that they will correspond to the buttons.

work even (straight): Continue in the established pattern without working any shaping.

working in pat: Follow the instructions for the pattern, whether written or graphed.

work in rounds: In circular knitting, the process of working a piece in which the ends have been joined and there are no seams.

working needle: The needle being used to make new stitches.

working yarn: The yarn being used to make new stitches.

work rep of chart . . . times: When working a pattern from a chart, work the stitches in the repeat as many times as indicated.

work to correspond: A term used when instructions are given for one piece, and a similar second piece must be made to correspond. There are usually some exceptions on the second piece, such as reversing shaping or pattern placement.

work to end: Work the established pattern to the end of the row.

work to . . . sts before center: Work the row to a specified number of stitches before the center of the row, which is generally indicated by a stitch marker.

work to last . . . sts: Work across the row until the specified number of stitches remains on the left needle.

work until . . . sts from bind-off (or on RH needle): After binding off, work until the specified number of stitches remains on the right needle.

wrong side (or WS): Usually refers to the surface of the work that will face inside when the garment is worn.

SYMBOLCRAFT

Symbolcraft is a universal form of knitting instructions. Instead of writing out a stitch pattern with words and abbreviations, symbols are used.

Each symbol represents the stitch as it appears on the right side of the work. For example, the symbol for a knit stitch is a vertical line and the symbol for a purl stitch is a horizontal one. On right-side rows, work the stitches as they appear on the chart—knitting the vertical lines and purling the horizontal ones. When reading wrong-side rows, work the opposite of what is shown; that is, purl the vertical lines and knit the horizontal ones.

In symbolcraft charts, each square represents one stitch and each line of squares equals one row. The rows are read from bottom to top. Usually, the odd-numbered rows are

Symbolcraft chart

Selvage or edge stitch.

St st: Stockinette stitch (knit on RS, purl on WS).

rev St st: Reverse stockinette stitch (purl on RS, knit on WS).

yo: Yarn over.

twisted St st: Knit stitch through back loop on RS; purl stitch through back loop on WS.

twisted rev St st: Purl stitch through back loop on RS; knit stitch through back loop on WS.

sl st knitwise: With yarn in back, slip stitch knitwise on RS; with yarn in front, slip stitch knitwise on WS.

sl st purlwise: With yarn in back, slip stitch purlwise on RS; with yarn in front, slip stitch purlwise on WS.

sl st purlwise (to create a float): With yarn in front, slip stitch purlwise on RS; with yarn in back, slip stitch purlwise on WS.

k1-b: Knit stitch in row below on RS; **p1-b:** purl stitch in row below on WS.

p1-b: Purl stitch in row below on RS; **k1-b:** knit stitch in row below on WS.

m1: Make one stitch as follows: On RS, insert left needle from front to back under horizontal strand between stitch just worked and next stitch on left needle. Knit this strand through the back loop. On WS, insert left needle from back to front under strand as before and purl it through back loop.

Make one stitch to form an eyelet as follows: On RS, insert left needle from front to back under horizontal strand between stitch just worked and next stitch on left needle. Knit this strand. On WS, insert left needle from back to front under strand as before and purl it.

inc 1 st: Increase one stitch as follows: Knit in front then in back of stitch on RS; purl in back then in front on WS.

Increase one stitch to the right as follows: With right needle, pick up next stitch on left needle in row below. Place loop on left needle and knit it.

Increase one stitch to the left as follows: With left needle, pick up next stitch on right needle one row below and knit it.

Increase three stitches in two as follows: Insert right needle knitwise into next two stitches on left needle. Knit one, purl one, knit one. Drop loops off left needle.

k2tog: On RS, knit two stitches together. **p2tog:** On WS, purl two stitches together.

listed on the right-hand side of the chart. Unless otherwise stated, these are always right-side rows and read horizontally from right to left. The numbers on the left-hand side of the chart are wrong-side rows, and are read from left to right. If you are working on a circular needle in rounds, you would read all the rows from right to left.

Sometimes only a single repeat of the pattern is charted. But if the pattern is complex, more than one repeat will be shown so that you can see how the finished motif will look. Heavy lines are usually drawn through the entire chart to indicate the repeat. These lines are the equivalent of an asterisk (*) or brackets [ ] used in written instructions.

Symbolcraft chart

SKP: On RS, slip one stitch. Knit next stitch and pass slip stitch over knit stitch. On WS, slip next two stitches knitwise. Slip these two stitches back to left needle without twisting them and purl them together through the back loops.

ssk: On RS, slip next two stitches knitwise. Insert tip of left needle into fronts of these two stitches and knit them together. On WS, slip one stitch, purl one stitch, then pass slip stitch over purl stitch.

p2tog: On RS, purl two stitches together. **k2tog:** On WS, knit two stitches together.

p2tog tbl: On RS, purl two stitches together through the back loops. **k2tog tbl:** on WS, knit two stitches together through back loops.

k3tog: On RS, knit three stitches together. **p3tog:** On WS, purl three stitches together.

p3tog: On RS, purl three stitches together. **k3tog:** On WS, knit three stitches together.

sk2p: On RS, slip one stitch, knit two stitches together. Pass slipped stitch over two stitches knit together. On WS, slip two stitches to right needle as if knitting two together. Slip next stitch knitwise. Slip all stitches to left needle without twisting them. Purl these three stitches together through back loops.

k4tog: On RS, knit four stitches together. **p4tog:** On WS, purl four stitches together.

dot-knot stitch: Insert RH needle from front to back under horizontal strand between 1st and 2nd sts on LH needle, wrap yarn and draw through a loop loosely; insert RH needle between same sts above horizontal strand, draw through another loop loosely; bring yarn

to front between needles and purl the first st on LH needle; with point of LH needle, pass the 1st loop over the 2nd loop and the purled st and off needle; pass the 2nd loop over the purled st and off needle.

peppercorn st: K next st, [sl st just knit back to LH needle and knit it again tbl] 3 times.

make bobble: [K1, p1] twice into next st, turn, p4, turn, k4, turn [p2tog] twice, turn, k2tog.

make bobble: [K1, p1, k1, p1, k1] in the same st, making 5 sts from one; then pass the 4th, 3rd, 2nd, and 1st sts over last st made.

make bobble: [K1, p1] 3 times, k1 in one st (7 sts made), then pass 2nd, 3rd, 4th, 5th, 6th, and 7th sts over last st made.

Symbolcraft: cables

2-st right twist: On RS rows, k2tog leaving sts on LH needle, k first st again, sl both sts from needle. On WS rows, wyif skip next st and purl the 2nd st, then purl skipped st, sl both sts from needle tog.

2-st left twist: With RH needle behind LH needle, skip the first st and k 2nd st tbl, insert RH needle into backs of both sts, k2tog tbl.

2-st right purl twist: Sl 1 st to cn and hold to back of work, k1, p1 from cn.

2-st left purl twist: Sl 1 st to cn and hold to front of work, p1, k1 from cn.

3-st right twist: Sl 2 sts to cn and hold to back of work, k1, then k2 from cn.

3-st left twist: Sl 1 st to cn and hold to front of work, k2, k1 from cn.

3-st right cable: Sl 1 st to cn and hold to back of work, k2, k1 from cn.

3-st left cable: Sl 2 sts to cn and hold to front of work, k1, k2 from cn.

3-st right purl cable: Sl 1 st to cn and hold to back of work, k2, p1 from cn.

3-st left purl cable: Sl 2 sts to cn and hold to front of work, p1, k2 from cn.

4-st right cable: Sl 2 sts to cn and hold to back of work, k2, k2 from cn.

4-st left cable: Sl 2 sts to cn and hold to front of work, k2, k2 from cn.

4-st right purl cable: Sl 1 st to cn and hold to back of work, p3, k1 from cn.

4-st left purl cable: Sl 3 sts to cn and hold to front of work, k1, p3 from cn.

4-st right purl cable: Sl 1 st to cn and hold to back of work, k3, p1 from cn.

4-st left purl cable: Sl 3 sts to cn and hold to front of work, p1, k3 from cn.

4-st wrap: Wyib sl 4, wyif sl same 4 sts to LH needle, wyib sl same 4 sts.

5-st right cable: Sl 3 sts to cn and hold to back of work, k2, sl purl st from cn to LH needle and purl it, k2 from cn.

5-st right purl cable: Sl 2 sts to cn and hold to back of work, k3, p2 from cn.

5-st left purl cable: Sl 3 sts to cn and hold to front of work, p2, k3 from cn.

tie st: Sl 5 sts to cn and hold to back of work, wrap yarn around these 5 sts 3 times, return sts to LH needle, then work them as foll: k1, p3, k1.

6-st right cable: Sl 3 sts to cn and hold to back of work, k3, k3 from cn.

6-st left cable: Sl 3 sts to cn and hold to front of work, k3, k3 from cn.

wrapped sts: K2, p2, k2, sl the last 6 sts worked onto cn and wrap yarn 4 times counterclockwise around these 6 sts; then sl the 6 sts back to RH needle.

12-st right cable: Sl 6 sts to cn and hold to back of work, k6, k6 from cn.

12-st left cable: Sl 6 sts to cn and hold to front of work, k6, k6 from cn.

III. Correcting Errors

CORRECTING ERRORS

Learning to correct mistakes is as necessary to knitting as learning to knit and purl—and most errors are easy to rectify. Some common problems for beginners include stitches that are backward, unwanted, dropped, or incomplete. If you are a beginner, check your work often because it is easiest to correct mistakes soon after you've made them.

If you have worked only a row or two beyond the error, you can work back to it stitch by stitch. If you don't discover the error until you have worked many rows, you must unravel to the mistake and rework from that point. However, you may be able to drop individual stitches above the error and unravel or "ladder" them back to the mistake, instead of unraveling several rows.

To unravel, use a contrasting yarn or stitch marker to mark the row with the error. Remove the knitting needle and pull out the stitches to that row. When working an intricate stitch pattern, keep track of the number of rows you unravel so that you won't lose your place.

After unraveling, put the stitches back onto a smaller needle—it will be easier to slip it into the loops. Make sure that the stitches are not backward as you return them to the needle. Work the stitches on the next row with the correct needle size.

Remember that certain novelty yarns and mohair are not easy to unravel. Use scissors to gently snip the hairs of fuzzy yarns as you unravel.

TWISTED STITCHES—KNIT AND PURL

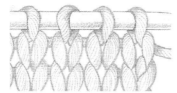

A twisted or backward stitch is created either by wrapping the yarn incorrectly on the previous row or by dropping a stitch and returning it to the needle backward.

To correct the backward knit stitch, knit it through the back loop.

A backward purl stitch looks different from a regular purl stitch in that the back loop is nearer the tip of the needle than the front loop.

To correct the backward purl stitch, purl it through the back loop.

PICKING UP A DROPPED KNIT STITCH

1 This method is used when a knit stitch has dropped only one row. Work to where the stitch was dropped. Be sure that the loose strand is behind the dropped stitch.

2 Insert the right needle from front to back into the dropped stitch and under the loose horizontal strand behind.

3 Insert the left needle from the back into the dropped stitch on the right needle, and pull this stitch over the loose strand.

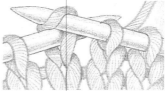

4 Transfer this newly made stitch back to the left needle by inserting the left needle from front to back into the stitch and slipping it off the right needle.

PICKING UP A DROPPED PURL STITCH

1 This method is used when a purl stitch has been dropped only one row. Work to the dropped purl stitch. Be sure that the loose horizontal strand is in front of the dropped stitch.

2 Insert the right needle from back to front into the dropped stitch, and then under the loose horizontal strand.

3 With the left needle, lift the dropped stitch over the horizontal strand and off the right needle.

4 Transfer the newly made purl stitch back to the left needle by inserting the left needle from front to back into the stitch and slipping it off the right needle.

PICKING UP A RUNNING KNIT AND PURL STITCH

A running stitch is one that has dropped more than one row. It is easiest to pick it up with a crochet hook. For a knit stitch, be sure the loose horizontal strands are in back of the dropped stitch.

Insert the hook into the stitch from front to back. Catch the first horizontal strand and pull it through. Continue up until you have worked all the strands. Place the newest stitch on the left needle, making sure it is not backward.

Before picking up a dropped purl stitch several rows below, be sure that the loose horizontal strands are in front of the stitch.

Insert the hook into the stitch from back to front. Pull the loose strand through the stitch. Continue up until you have worked all the strands. Place the newest stitch on the left needle, making sure it is not backward.

INCOMPLETE KNIT AND PURL STITCHES

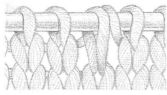

An incomplete knit or purl stitch is one where the yarn is wrapped around the needle but not pulled through the stitch. The illustration above shows an incomplete stitch from the previous purl row.

Work to the incomplete stitch. Insert the right needle from back to front into the stitch on the left needle and pull it over the strand and off the needle.

This illustration shows an incomplete stitch from the previous knit row.

Insert the right needle into the stitch on the left needle and pull it over the strand and off the needle.

AN EXTRA STITCH AT THE EDGE

If you bring the yarn back over the top of the needle at the beginning of the knit row, the first stitch will have two loops instead of one, as shown.

To avoid creating this extra stitch, keep the yarn under the needle when taking it to the back to knit the first stitch.

At the beginning of a purl row, if the yarn is at the back, and then brought to the front under the needle, the first stitch will have two loops instead of one, as shown.

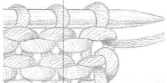

To avoid making these two loops, the yarn should be at the front before you purl the first stitch.

UNRAVELING STITCH BY STITCH

Knit stitches Keep the yarn at the back. Insert the left needle into the stitch one row below the stitch on the right needle. Drop the stitch and pull the yarn to undo it.

Purl stitches Keep the yarn at the front. Insert the left needle into the stitch one row below the stitch on the right needle. Drop the stitch and pull the yarn to undo it.

UNRAVELING ROWS

If you need to unravel one or more rows, you must put the stitches back onto the needle correctly. Make sure the working yarn is at the left side. Using a smaller needle, insert it from back to front into each stitch across the row.

To put purl stitches back on the needle after unraveling them, first make sure the working yarn is at the left side. Insert a smaller needle from front to back into each stitch across the row.

If you are concerned about dropping stitches, you can weave the right needle under the first loop and over the second loop of each knit stitch along the entire row. Pull the working yarn to unravel all the stitches above those on the needle.

You can also use this method with purl stitches. Insert the needle under the first loop and over the second loop of each purl stitch along the entire row. Pull the working yarn to unravel all the stitches.

IV. CIRCULAR AND DOUBLE-POINTED KNITTING

Circular Needles

When knitting on circular needles, you can join the work to make tubular pieces or work back and forth as with straight needles. Actually, many knitters prefer circular needles when knitting flat pieces, especially with a large number of stitches, since the stitches and the weight of the knitting are evenly distributed.

Circular needles are available in several lengths. The length that you use will depend on the number of stitches you will be working with and the stitch gauge. The needle should be short enough so that the stitches are not stretched when joined. The needle can accommodate up to four times the original number of stitches, so you may not have to change needle length when you increase stitches above the rib.

Circular needles are available with plastic, aluminum, or Teflon-coated tips, but all have plastic joining wires. If the plastic wire portion of the needle curls, immerse it in hot water to straighten it before you begin to knit.

When you join your work, make sure that the stitches are not twisted around the needle. A twisted cast-on can't be rectified once you have worked a round. To help you keep the stitches untwisted, keep the cast-on edge facing the center, or work one row before joining the stitches, then sew the gap closed later.

To identify the beginning of each new round, place a marker between the first and last cast-on stitches before joining. Slip the marker to the right hand needle before each subsequent round.

Casting on and Knitting

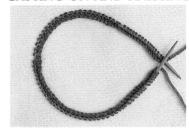

Cast on as you would for straight knitting. Distribute the stitches evenly around the needle, being sure not to twist them. The last cast-on stitch is the last stitch of the round. Place a marker here to indicate the end of the round.

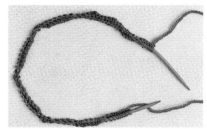

If the cast-on stitches are twisted, as shown, you will find that after you knit a few inches the fabric will be twisted. You will have to rip out your work to the cast-on row and straighten the stitches.

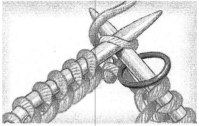

1 Hold the needle tip with the last cast-on stitch in your right hand and the tip with the first cast-on stitch in your left hand. Knit the first cast-on stitch, pulling the yarn tight to avoid a gap.

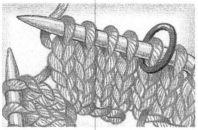

2 Work until you reach the marker. This completes the first round. Slip the marker to the right needle and work the next round.

DOUBLE-POINTED NEEDLES

Double-pointed needles have points at both ends and come in sets of four or five needles in seven-inch (18cm) and ten-inch (25cm) lengths.

Unlike circular needles, they are used only for tubular pieces. Actually, the very first circular knitting was done on double-pointed needles. Since the invention of circular needles, double-pointed needles are used less often, usually to knit small items such as mittens, gloves, socks, hats, and sleeve cuffs.

The stitches are divided evenly among three or four needles. An extra needle is used to knit the stitches. When your work is joined on three needles, the needles form a triangle. When joined on four needles, a square is formed. Make sure that you keep an even tension when going from one needle to the next. If you find that your stitches slip off the needles as you work, choose longer double-pointed needles or switch to a circular needle.

On the first round, you can work the first few stitches with both the working yarn and the cast-on tail to create a neater joining. Another way to make a neat joining is to cast on one extra stitch on the last needle. Slip this stitch to the first needle and knit it together with the first cast-on stitch.

Just as for circular needles, you should mark the beginning of the round, and take care to make sure that the cast-on edge is not twisted.

On the last round, use the free needle to bind off the stitches on the first needle until one stitch remains. Drop the free needle and use the needle with the one remaining stitch to bind off the stitches on the next needle to the last stitch. Continue in this way to the last stitch on the last needle and fasten off this stitch.

CASTING ON AND KNITTING

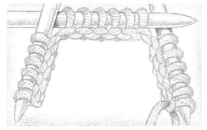

Cast-on with three needles.

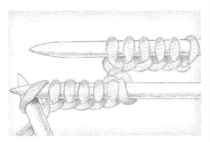

1 Cast on the required number of stitches on the first needle, plus one extra. Slip this extra stitch to the next needle as shown. Continue in this way, casting on the required number of stitches on the last needle.

2 Arrange the needles as shown, with the cast-on edge facing the center of the triangle (or square).

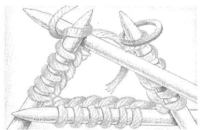

3 Place a stitch marker after the last cast-on stitch. With the free needle, knit the first cast-on stitch, pulling the yarn tightly. Continue knitting in rounds, slipping the marker before beginning each round.

SOCK BASICS

Socks, or "stockings," as some still call them, have been knit for hundreds of years all around the world. In many countries, children are taught to knit socks at a young age. To those without the benefit of this experience, sock knitting may appear sophisticated. Actually, "turning" a heel is an easy skill to master, and the excitement of seeing the heel develop adds a certain momentum to sock knitting. Socks can be constructed in all manners—knit in the round on double-pointed needles or knit flat and then seamed—and just about any type of patterning can be incorporated into a sock's design.

While most socks these days are knit from patterns that may feature any number of design elements and varia-tions in techniques, certain aspects of their construction remain consistent. The following information describes the basic components of socks and offers some notes on how they are made.

SOCK CONSTRUCTION

Most socks are knit in the round on a set of four or five double-pointed needles. This eliminates seams at heels and toes, making the socks more comfortable for the wearer.

The toes, and in some designs, the heels, are woven together using the kitchener stitch. The kitchener stitch mimics a knit stitch, is neat, and provides an invisible seam.

Cuff: Most socks are worked from the top down, beginning with the cuff.

The desired number of stitches are cast on to one needle, then divided equally over three or four needles to work in rounds. This helps keep the stitches from twisting on the first round. For most socks, the number of stitches on the cuff will equal the number of stitches on the foot after the heel and instep shaping are completed. Cuffs often begin with one-and-a-half to two-and-a-half inches (3.5cm to 6cm) of ribbing for extra elasticity at the top of the sock, though some socks may be ribbed the entire length of the cuff, and others may be topped with a lace or other stitch pattern, and feature no ribbing at all.

Heel: After the cuff is the desired length, usually five to seven inches (12.5cm to 17.5cm), the number of

Adapting stitch patterns

Most patterns are written for straight, single-pointed needles. However, you can often adapt them to circular knitting by making a few adjustments to the pattern.

The most important point to remember is that the right side of the work is always facing you. This means that if you knit every row, you get stockinette stitch. To work garter stitch you must alternate one knit row with one purl row.

If the existing pattern has stitches outside of the pattern repeat, you will have to add or subtract from the total number of stitches to come up with a multiple of the stitch repeat.

If the pattern is charted, read all the rows from right to left. If the pattern is written out, work the right-side rows as written, but reverse the wrong-side rows by reading them from right to left and working the opposite stitches. For example, for straight knitting the pattern reads: *Row 2 (WS)* K2, sl 1 wyib, k2, p3. For circular knitting the row should read: K3, p2, sl 1 wyif, p2. It is helpful to write out all the wrong-side rows before you begin.

stitches is generally divided in half and shifted around the needles so that the center of the heel is at the beginning of the cuff rounds. The remaining instep stitches—those that make up the front of the foot—are divided onto two needles to be worked later.

The heel is then worked straight on two needles (that is, back and forth in rows), until it is the desired depth. The heel is then shaped—or "turned," as it is commonly described—with short rows into a V-shape or a curved U-shape. The techniques used to turn a heel vary somewhat; your pattern will tell you which method to use for the sock you are knitting.

Instep: To begin working in rounds again, as well as to join the instep to the heel, stitches are knit and repositioned again so that the round begins at the center of the heel (now, the sole of the foot). Stitches are picked up and knit along each side of the heel piece; these stitches will become part of the instep. In subsequent rounds, these stitches will be decreased on either side of the foot (usually on the first and third needles) until the original number of stitches in the round is reached. This decreasing shapes the instep into a wedge shape, sometimes called a gusset, which fits the shape of the wearer's foot as it, too, decreases in width from the heel.

Foot: When the instep shaping is complete, the foot is worked straight, with no further shaping, until the sock foot measures two inches (5cm) less than the desired length from the end of the heel to the end of the toe. When working the foot, original stitch or color patterns established in the cuff are resumed; however, in some cases, highly textured stitch patterns, such as ribs or some lace patterns, are eliminated from the sole of the foot to ensure greater comfort for the wearer.

Toe: Once again, if the stitches are not already in the correct alignment, they are shifted so that half the stitches are on needle 2 and the other half of the stitches are divided onto needles 1 and 3. Then double decreases are worked at each side edge of the toe until the required number of remaining stitches is reached. The toe stitches are then woven together with kitchener stitch, and the sock is complete.

Sock Sizing

Sock sizing is as individual as shoe sizing. The best approach to fitting a sock is to measure the foot of the wearer (from the end of the heel to the end of the toe) and knit the foot length accordingly. A good rule of thumb is to begin the toe shaping when the foot of the sock reaches the base of the little toe of the wearer—approximately two inches (5cm) down from the tip of the big toe.

Sock Yarn

Socks are most frequently made with wool or a wool blend, though cotton or cotton-wool blends work well, too. Wool provides warmth and wicks moisture away from skin, making it an ideal fiber for socks. Unlike cotton, wool also has a natural elasticity, allowing for socks that hold their shape well and fit snugly.

When making socks with wool, however, it is wise to choose a wool yarn that also contains a small percentage of nylon, which provides added strength for areas that will receive extra wear, like heels and toes. Alternately, a reinforcement yarn—usually a very thin wool-nylon blend—can be added to a pure wool when knitting the areas of a sock that require extra strength.

Cotton is absorbent, cool, and ideal for warm-weather socks. Because of its lack of elasticity, however, you may want to pair it with a sock pattern that features a fully ribbed cuff, to ensure a snug fit.

Socks can be made with nearly any weight of yarn—the most common choices are fingering or sock weight, DK or sport weight, and worsted weight. As with any knitted item, the thicker the yarn used, the larger the needles required, and the fewer stitches needed to achieve the same circumference.

Fingering: Socks made with fingering or sock yarn will have a fine gauge, and will be thin enough to wear with most any shoe. For an average-sized sock with a seven-inch (17.5cm) cuff, you will need approximately 200 yards (183m) of fingering-weight yarn per sock. Most fingering-weight yarn manufactured specifically for socks comes in skeins of 180 to 250 yards (165m to 229m), enough for one sock each. Be sure to purchase two for a pair.

Sport: Knitting with DK- or sport-weight yarn will result in slightly heavier socks, usually wearable with casual shoes. For an average-sized sock with a seven-inch (17.5cm) cuff, you will need approximately 175 yards (160m) of sport-weight yarn per sock.

Worsted: Socks made with worsted-weight yarn will be quite heavy and thick, and are often referred to as boot socks. For an average-sized sock with a seven-inch (17.5cm) cuff, you will need approximately 140 yards (128m) of worsted-weight yarn per sock.

V. Color Knitting

Fair Isle Knitting

Stranding: One-handed

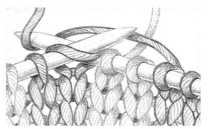

1 On the knit side, drop the working yarn. Bring the new color (now the working yarn) over the top of the dropped yarn and work to the next color change.

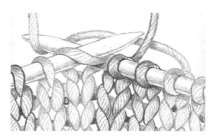

2 Drop the working yarn. Bring the new color under the dropped yarn and work to the next color change. Repeat steps 1 and 2.

1 On the purl side, drop the working yarn. Bring the new color (now the working yarn) over the top of the dropped yarn and work to the next color change.

2 Drop the working yarn. Bring the new color under the dropped yarn and work to the next color change. Repeat steps 1 and 2.

Stranding: Two-handed

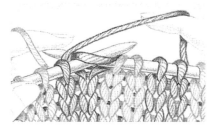

1 On the knit side, hold the working yarn in your right hand and the non-working yarn in your left hand. Bring the working yarn over the top of the yarn in your left hand and knit with the right hand to the next color change.

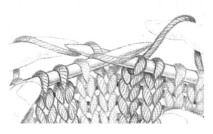

2 The yarn in your right hand is now the non-working yarn; the yarn in your left hand is the working yarn. Bring the working yarn under the non-working yarn and knit with the left hand to the next color change. Repeat steps 1 and 2.

1 On the purl side, hold the working yarn in your right hand and the non-working yarn in your left hand. Bring the working yarn over the top of the yarn in your left hand and purl with the right hand to the next color change.

2 The yarn in your right hand is now the non-working yarn; the yarn in your left hand is the working yarn. Bring the working yarn under the non-working yarn and purl with the left hand to the next color change. Repeat steps 1 and 2.

WEAVING

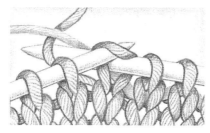

1 Hold the working yarn in your right hand and the yarn to be woven in your left. To weave the yarn above a knit stitch, bring it over the right needle. Knit the stitch with the working yarn, bringing it under the woven yarn.

2 The woven yarn will go under the next knit stitch. With the working yarn, knit the stitch, bringing the yarn over the woven yarn. Repeat steps 1 and 2 to the next color change.

1 To weave the yarn above a purl stitch, bring it over the right needle. Purl the stitch with the working yarn, bringing it under the woven yarn.

2 To weave the yarn below a purl stitch, purl the stitch with the working yarn, bringing it over the woven yarn. Repeat steps 1 and 2 to the next color change.

TWISTING

On the knit side, twist the working yarn and the carried yarn around each other once. Then continue knitting with the same color as before.

On the purl side, twist the yarns around each other as shown, then continue purling with the same color as before.

Intarsia

Intarsia is a colorwork technique in which blocks of color are worked with separate balls of yarn or bobbins. The yarns are not carried across the back of the work between color changes and must be twisted around each other at each change to prevent holes in the work.

Intarsia knitting should not be worked circularly because at the end of the round, the yarns would be in the wrong position. You would have to cut all the yarn and reattach it, leaving you to weave in hundreds of ends.

When changing colors in a vertical line, the yarns must be twisted on every row. When changing colors in a diagonal line, the yarns must only be twisted on every other row. If the diagonal slants to the right, twist the yarns only on knit rows. If the diagonal slants to the left, twist the yarns only on purl rows.

Changing colors in a vertical line

 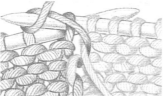

1 On the knit side, drop the old color. Pick up the new color from under the old color and knit to the next color change.

2 On the purl side, drop the old color. Pick up the new color from under the old color and purl to the next color change. Repeat steps 1 and 2.

Changing colors in a diagonal line

1 When working a right diagonal on the knit side, bring the new color over the top of the old color and knit to the next color change.

2 On the purl side, pick up the new color from under the old color and purl to the next color change.

1 When working a left diagonal on the purl side, bring the new color over the top of the old color and purl to the next color change.

2 On the knit side, pick up the new color from under the old color and knit to the next color change.

JOINING A NEW COLOR: VERSION A

1 Wrap first the old and then the new yarn knitwise and work the first stitch with both yarns.

2 Drop the old yarn. Work the next two stitches with both ends of the new yarn.

3 Drop the short end of the new color and continue working with the single strand. On the following rows, work the three double stitches as single stitches.

JOINING A NEW COLOR: VERSION B

1 Cut the old yarn, leaving about four inches (10cm). Purl the first two stitches with the new yarn. *Insert the needle purlwise into the stitch, lay the short ends of both the old and new colors over the top of the needle, and purl the next stitch under the short ends.

2 Leave the short ends hanging and purl the next stitch over them.

3 Repeat from the * until you have woven the short ends into the wrong side of the piece.

Intarsia continued

Joining a new color: version C

1 Work to three stitches before where you want to join the new yarn. Work these stitches with the yarn folded double, making sure you have just enough to work three stitches.

2 Loop the new yarn into the loop of the old yarn, leaving the new yarn doubled for about eight inches (20cm). Knit the next three stitches with the doubled yarn. Let the short end of the new yarn hang and continue knitting with one strand.

3 On the next row, carry the first yarn across the back of the work from where it was dropped on the previous row and twist it together with the second yarn. Work the doubled stitches as single stitches.

Horizontal Stripes

Horizontal stripes are one of the easiest types of color knitting, since you do not have to carry yarns across the row as you work. You can cut the yarn as you finish each stripe, but this means weaving in many ends after the pieces are complete. To avoid this, carry the yarns you are not using along the side of the work.

If working a stripe pattern back and forth, you should have an even number of rows in each stripe, so that the yarn will be at the correct side of the work when you need it. If the pattern calls for odd-numbered stripes, you will have to cut the yarn and rejoin it on the opposite side. To avoid this, you can change the pattern to make an even number of rows in each stripe. You can also work the piece back and forth on a circular needle. If you complete a stripe and need to change to the new color, but the yarn is at the opposite side, go back to the beginning of the row you just finished, without turning the work, and pick up the color you need. If you are knitting the garment circularly, it does not matter how many rows are in the stripes, as you are always working right-side rows.

When you change colors on the right side of the work, and you purl with the new color on top of knit stitches in the old color, you will get a broken line. To avoid this, knit one row with the new color.

Carrying Colors Along the Side

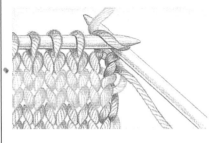

1 When changing colors with narrow, even-numbered stripes, drop the old color. Bring the new color under the old color, being sure not to pull the yarn too tightly, and knit the next stripe.

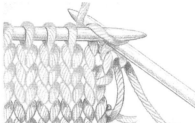

2 When working thicker stripes (generally more than four rows), carry the old yarn up the side until it is needed again by twisting the working yarn around the old yarn every couple of rows, as shown.

Vertical Stripes

When working vertical stripes, you must either carry the colors across the back of the work or use separate balls or bobbins for each stripe. If each stripe has four or fewer stitches, carry the yarns across the back. With more than four, use bobbins and twist the colors around each other on every row.

To make a vertical stripe of one stitch in stockinette, knit the piece in the main color, then duplicate stitch the stripe onto it.

If you want the stripes to start at the beginning of the piece, cast on with only one color, then start the stripes on the first row. Or you can cast on using the colors in the stripes, as shown below.

A corrugated rib is ribbing made of vertical stripes in knit and purl stitches. While it does make an interesting effect, it does not have the same give as solid-color ribbing and should be made slightly wider to compensate for its lack of resiliency. It is best worked in knit one, purl one or knit two, purl two ribbing. Remember to always twist the colors on the wrong side of the work to prevent holes.

Casting on for Vertical Stripes

1 Using the double cast-on, and with the end of the yarn coming from the skein over your thumb, cast on the first color. Make a slip knot on the needle with the second color. To cast on the second stitch, twist the old and new colors, as shown.

2 If working in stockinette stitch, purl the first wrong-side row, twisting the yarns at each color change, as shown. Pull the yarn tightly to prevent gaps.

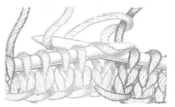

3 On the second (knit) row, twist the yarns by bringing the working yarn over the old yarn.

Corrugated Ribbing

1 On the right side, before a purl stitch, drop the old color. Bring the working color under the old color and to the front of the work between the needles. Purl the next two stitches.

2 Before a knit stitch, bring the old color to the back of the work and leave it. Bring the working color under the old color and knit the next two stitches.

1 On the wrong side, before a knit stitch, drop the old color. Bring the working color over the top of the old color and to the back of the work as shown. Knit the next two stitches.

2 Before a purl stitch, drop the old color, bring the working color over the top of the old color, and purl the next two stitches.

VI. Assembling

SEAMING

You can choose from many types of seaming techniques, depending on your personal preference. Each method has its own characteristics and may require different tools.

It is best to use your knitting yarn to sew the pieces together, unless you have used a novelty or untwisted, roving yarn. In that case, sew the seams with a flat, firm yarn in a compatible color. Be sure that it has the same washability as your knitting yarn.

Block your pieces before you sew them together to make the edges smoother and easier to seam. Pin or baste the seams before final seaming. Try the garment on and make sure that it fits properly.

Attach any small items, such as pockets or embroidery, before seaming, as it is easier to work with one piece than the entire garment.

Most knitters follow this sequence when seaming a garment: Sew one or both shoulder seams, depending on the type of garment and the method you'll use to add any neckband. Sew the sleeves to the body, and then sew the side and sleeve seams.

As you seam, try to keep an even tension. Pull the yarn firmly as you go but not so tightly that the edges will pucker.

Do not use too long a piece of yarn when seaming—no more than 18 inches (46cm). The constant friction of the yarn through the knitting can cause the yarn to break.

Be sure to keep the seam in a neat, straight line. Always insert your needle in the same place along the seam. If necessary, run a contrasting thread through the stitches or rows to help you see the line more clearly.

If the two pieces you are seaming are slightly different lengths, you can compensate by picking up two rows or stitches on the longer side every few inches. This can only work if the difference is no more than one-half inch (1.5cm). If it is any more than that, you must rework one of the pieces.

Any edges that will be turned back, such as cuffs or a turtleneck, should be seamed from the opposite side so that the seam will not show when the edge is turned.

How to begin seaming

If you have left a long tail from your cast-on row, you can use this strand to begin sewing. To make a neat join at the lower edge with no gap, use the technique shown here. Thread the strand into a yarn needle. With the right sides of both pieces facing you, insert the yarn needle from back to front into the corner stitch of the piece without the tail. Making a figure eight with the yarn, insert the needle from back to front into the stitch with the cast-on tail. Tighten to close the gap.

Invisible Vertical on Stockinette Stitch

The invisible vertical seam is worked from the right side and is used to join two edges row by row. It hides the uneven selvage stitches at the edge of a row and creates an invisible seam, making it appear that the knitting is continuous.

The finished vertical seam on stockinette stitch.

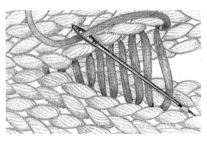

Insert the yarn needle under the horizontal bar between the first and second stitches. Insert the needle into the corresponding bar on the other piece. Continue alternating from side to side.

Invisible Vertical on Reverse Stockinette Stitch

As with stockinette stitch, this invisible seam is worked from the right side, row by row, but instead of working into the horizontal strand between stitches, you work into the stitch itself. Alternate working into the top loop on one side with the bottom loop on the other side.

The finished vertical seam on reverse stockinette stitch.

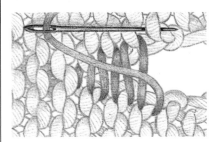

Working into the stitches inside the edge, insert the yarn needle into the top loop on one side, then in the bottom loop of the corresponding stitch on the other side. Continue to alternate in this way.

SEAMING CONTINUED

INVISIBLE VERTICAL ON GARTER STITCH

This invisible seam is worked on garter stitch. It is similar to the seam worked on reverse stockinette stitch in that you alternate working into the top and bottom loops of the stitches.

The finished vertical seam on garter stitch.

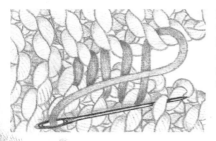

Insert the yarn needle into the top loop on one side, then in the bottom loop of the corresponding stitch on the other side. Continue to alternate in this way.

INVISIBLE HORIZONTAL

This seam is used to join two bound-off edges, such as shoulder seams, and is worked stitch by stitch. You must have the same number of stitches on each piece. Pull the yarn tight enough to hide the bound-off edges. The finished seam resembles a row of knit stitches.

The finished horizontal seam on stockinette stitch.

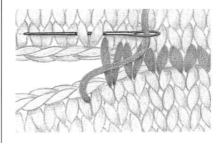

With the bound-off edges together, lined up stitch for stitch, insert the yarn needle under a stitch inside the bound-off edge of one side and then under the corresponding stitch on the other side.

INVISIBLE VERTICAL TO HORIZONTAL

This seam is used to join bound-off stitches to rows, as in sewing the top of a sleeve to an armhole edge. Since there are usually more rows per inch (2.5cm) than stitches, occasionally pick up two horizontal bars on the piece with rows for every stitch on the bound-off piece.

The finished vertical to horizontal seam on stockinette stitch.

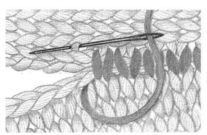

Insert the yarn needle under a stitch inside the bound-off edge of the vertical piece. Insert the needle under one or two horizontal bars between the first and second stitches of the horizontal piece.

BACKSTITCH

This is a strong seam that is worked from the wrong side and creates a seam allowance. Because it is not worked at the edge of the fabric, it can be used to take in fullness. The seam allowance should not exceed three-eighths inch (1cm).

The finished backstitch on stockinette stitch.

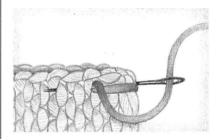

1 With the right sides of the pieces facing each other, secure the seam by taking the needle twice around the edges from back to front. Bring the needle up about one-fourth inch (.5cm) from where the yarn last emerged, as shown.

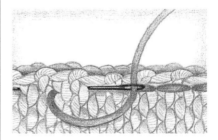

2 In one motion, insert the needle into the point where the yarn emerged from the previous stitch and back up approximately one-fourth inch (.5cm) ahead of the emerging yarn. Pull the yarn through. Repeat this step, keeping the stitches straight and even.

Seaming continued

Overcasting

This seam is usually worked from the wrong side, but it can also be worked from the right side with a thick yarn in a contrasting color to create a decorative, cord-like seam.

The finished overcast seam on stockinette stitch.

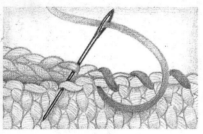

With the right sides of the pieces facing each other and the knots lined up, insert the needle from back to front through the strands at the edges of the pieces between the knots. Repeat this step.

Edge-to-edge

The edge-to-edge seam, being flat, is perfect for reversible garments. It is worked at the very edge of the piece. Because it is not a strong seam, it is best used with lightweight yarns.

The finished edge-to-edge seam on stockinette stitch.

The finished edge-to-edge seam on reverse stockinette stitch.

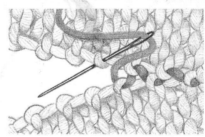

With the purl sides facing you and the edges of the pieces together, insert the yarn needle into the knot on one side, then into the corresponding knot on the other side.

Grafting

Grafting, also called weaving or kitchener stitch, joins two open edges stitch by stitch using a yarn needle. The grafted edges resemble a row of stitches and leave no seam. This makes grafting useful when a seam is undesirable, such as on mittens, hoods that may fold over, and the toes of socks.

Because you must follow the path of the stitches with the yarn needle, grafting is best used on simple stitches such as stockinette, reverse stockinette, or garter stitch, which have been worked in flat, smooth yarns, making the stitches clearly visible.

You should graft stitches together while they are still on the knitting needles, slipping a few off at a time as you work. Be sure that the needles are pointing in the same direction when the wrong sides of your work are placed together. In order to do this, you will need to work one row less on one needle or reverse one of the needles.

When grafting garter stitch, it is important that the purl stitches of the front piece face the knit stitches of the back piece.

Grafting on stockinette stitch (kitchener stitch)

A grafted seam on stockinette stitch.

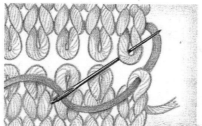

1 Insert the yarn needle purlwise into the first stitch on the front piece, then knitwise into the first stitch on the back piece. Draw the yarn through.

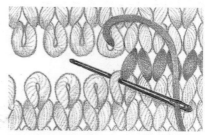

2 Insert the yarn needle knitwise into the first stitch on the front piece again. Draw the yarn through.

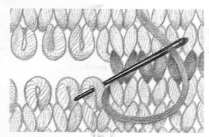

3 Insert the yarn needle purlwise into the next stitch on the front piece. Draw the yarn through.

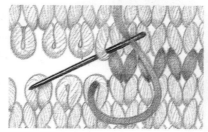

4 Insert the yarn needle purlwise into the first stitch on the back piece again. Draw the yarn through.

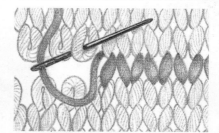

5 Insert the yarn needle knitwise into the next stitch on the back piece. Draw the yarn through. Repeat steps 2 through 5.

GRAFTING CONTINUED

GRAFTING ON GARTER STITCH

A grafted seam on garter stitch.

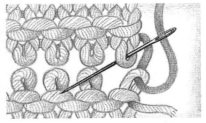

1 Insert the yarn needle purlwise into the first stitch on the front piece, then purlwise into the first stitch on the back piece. Draw the yarn through.

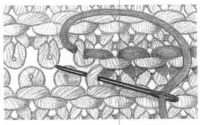

2 Insert the yarn needle knitwise into the first stitch on the front piece again. Draw the yarn through.

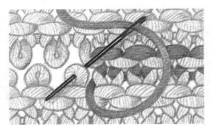

3 Insert the yarn needle purlwise into the next stitch on the front piece. Draw the yarn through.

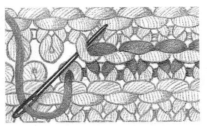

4 Insert the yarn needle knitwise into the first stitch on the back piece again. Draw the yarn through.

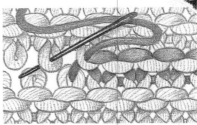

5 Insert the yarn needle purlwise into the next stitch on the back piece. Draw the yarn through. Repeat steps 2 through 5.

GRAFTING ON KNIT ONE, PURL ONE RIBBING

A grafted seam on knit one, purl one ribbing. You will need four double-pointed needles or circular needles for this technique.

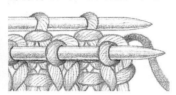

1 Separate the knit stitches from the purl stitches on each ribbed piece by slipping the knit stitches onto one needle and the purl stitches onto a second needle.

2 Graft all the knit stitches on one side of the piece as shown.

3 Turn the work. Graft all the knit stitches on the other side.

VERTICAL TO HORIZONTAL

A finished seam showing open stitches grafted to rows on stockinette stitch.

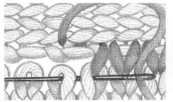

When grafting open stitches to rows, you must compensate for the difference in stitch and row gauge by occasionally picking up two horizontal bars for every stitch.

A finished seam showing open stitches grafted to rows on reverse stockinette stitch.

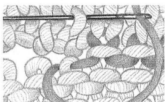

When grafting open stitches to rows in reverse stockinette stitch, pick up the loop of the purl stitch inside the edge, as shown.

GRAFTING CONTINUED

OPEN STITCHES TO BOUND-OFF STITCHES

A finished seam showing open stitches grafted to bound-off stitches on stockinette stitch.

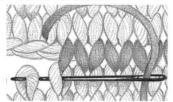

When grafting open stitches to bound-off stitches, insert the yarn needle under the stitch inside the bound-off edge and then into the corresponding stitch on the open edge.

A finished seam showing open stitches grafted to bound-off stitches on reverse stockinette stitch.

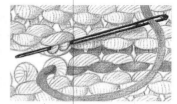

When grafting open stitches to bound-off stitches on reverse stockinette stitch, pick up two vertical strands just inside the bound-off edge, as shown.

Joining knit one, purl one ribbing

When joining ribbing with a purl stitch at each edge, insert the yarn needle under the horizontal bar in the center of a knit stitch on each side.

When joining ribbing with a knit stitch at each edge, use the bottom loop of the purl stitch on one side and the top loop of the corresponding purl stitch on the other side.

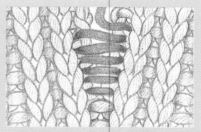

When joining purl and knit stitch edges, skip knit stitch and join two purl stitches as at left.

PICKING UP STITCHES

When you add any type of border, such as a neckband, to finished pieces, you generally pick up stitches along the edge. It is important that you do so evenly to make a smooth join between the edge and the border.

The neatest way to pick up stitches is to do it from the right side of the work. It is also important to actually make knit stitches on a knitting needle with a separate strand of yarn rather than picking up a strand from the edge of the piece itself, which will stretch and distort the edge.

Begin picking up by attaching the yarn to the edge of the piece, or simply start picking up, pulling on the short end to make sure the stitches do not unravel.

You can use a knitting needle (straight or circular) or a crochet hook to pick up stitches. Be sure that it is one or two sizes smaller than the needles used for the main body. The smaller size is easier to insert into the fabric and will not stretch the picked-up stitches. After picking up, change to the needle size used for the edging.

If the instructions do not tell you how many stitches to pick up, measure the total area and multiply that figure by the stitch gauge of the edging to be added. To determine the gauge of the edging, pick up and add the edging to your gauge swatch or make a separate piece using the pattern stitch for the edging. If you have already used the edging in the main body of the sweater, measure your gauge from that.

Along a shaped edge, such as a neck, make sure you pick up inside the edge so as not to create any holes.

If you are making a band in a different color from the main piece, pick up stitches with the main color, then change the color on the first row.

If you change the size of the sweater from the instructions, make sure you adjust the number of stitches to be picked up accordingly.

When you pick up stitches on a long piece, such as the entire outside edge of a cardigan, there may be too many stitches to fit on a straight, single-pointed needle. Divide the edge in half, working first along the right front to the center back neck and then from the center back neck along the left front. Then seam your edging at the back neck. Alternately, all of your stitches may fit on a long circular needle.

When picking up for a neckband on a pullover with a single-pointed needle, sew one shoulder seam. Pick up the stitches required, work the edging, then sew the second shoulder seam and the side of the neckband. If using circular or double-pointed needles, sew both shoulder seams, pick up the required stitches, join, and work the edging in rounds.

Marking edge for picking up stitches

Stitches must be picked up evenly so that the band will not flare or pull in. Place pins, markers, or yarn, as shown, every two inches (5cm) and pick up the same number of stitches between each pair of markers. If you know the number of stitches to be picked up, divide this by the number of sections to determine how many stitches to pick up in each one.

Picking Up Stitches CONTINUED

Horizontal edge with knitting needle

Stitches picked up along a bound-off edge.

1 Insert the knitting needle into the center of the first stitch in the row below the bound-off edge. Wrap the yarn knitwise around the needle.

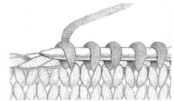

2 Draw the yarn through. You have picked up one stitch. Continue to pick up one stitch in each stitch along the bound-off edge.

Vertical edge with knitting needle

Stitches picked up along a side edge.

1 Insert the knitting needle into the corner stitch of the first row, one stitch in from the side edge. Wrap the yarn around the needle knitwise.

2 Draw the yarn through. You have picked up one stitch. Continue to pick up stitches along the edge. Occasionally skip one row to keep the edge from flaring.

Shaped edge with knitting needle

Stitches picked up along a curved edge.

Pick up stitches neatly just inside the shaped edge, following the curve and hiding the jagged selvage.

Stitches picked up along a diagonal edge.

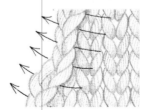

Pick up stitches one stitch in from the shaped edge, keeping them in a straight line.

PICKING UP ALONG A NECK EDGE

The stitches for this neckband are picked up around the V-neck using straight needles. Leave the right shoulder seam unsewn and begin picking up stitches at the right back neck. Work the neckband back and forth.

The stitches for this neckband are picked up around the V-neck using a circular needle. Sew both shoulders and begin picking up stitches at the right back neck. Place a marker and join the piece.

The stitches for this neckband are picked up around the V-neck using double-pointed needles. Sew both shoulders and begin picking up stitches at the right back neck. Use one needle for the back and one needle for each front. Place a marker and join the piece.

PICKING UP STITCHES WITH A CROCHET HOOK

1 Insert the crochet hook from front to back into the center of the first stitch one row below the bound-off edge. Catch the yarn and pull a loop through.

2 Slip the loop onto the knitting needle, being sure it is not twisted. Continue to pick up one stitch in each stitch along the bound-off edge.

The number of stitches to pick up

If the correct number of stitches are picked up, the finished edge will be straight and even.

If too few stitches are picked up, the finished edge will pull in.

If too many stitches are picked up, the finished edge will flare out.

How to Attach and Hem

Attaching

You can make separate pieces, such as collars or elaborate edgings, and attach them later. Since these seams often follow a curve, it is important to keep the stitches even.

When you sew the open stitches of a border to the finished edge of a garment, place the open stitches on a piece of contrasting yarn to keep them from unraveling. Remove the contrasting yarn a few stitches at a time while seaming.

Hemming

When securing a knitted-in hem, it is important that your stitching leaves no visible line on the right side of your garment.

Fold the hem to the wrong side (along the turning ridge if one has been worked) and carefully pin it in place. Be sure that it is hemmed in a straight line. Do not pull the yarn tightly or the work will pucker.

You can hem with various types of stitches. The whip stitch is best used on medium- or lightweight yarns. It creates a neat and firm seam. The stitch-by-stitch method is good for bulky yarns, as you eliminate a bulky cast-on edge by grafting open stitches to the back of the work.

Slip stitching a pocket

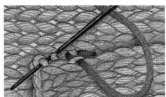

When attaching a separate piece, such as a patch pocket, to the knitted fabric, pick up the horizontal bar in the center of a stitch from the fabric, then the horizontal bar one stitch in from the pocket edge. Draw the yarn through.

Whip stitch on a hem

Fold the hem to the wrong side, being sure that the stitches are straight. Insert the needle into a stitch on the wrong side of the fabric and then into the cast-on edge of the hem. Draw the yarn through.

Herringbone stitch on a hem

Working from left to right, attach the yarn to the upper left corner of the hem. Tack the cast-on edge of the hem to the fabric using the herringbone stitch as shown.

Backstitching and slip stitching a neckband

You can join open stitches of a neckband by backstitching them to the neck edge from the right side.

Backstitch instead of binding off the stitches of a band. Place the open stitches onto a contrasting yarn. Sew the stitches to the neck edge from the right side of the work using the backstitch as shown.

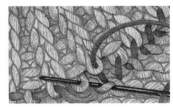

Slip stitch if working a doubled neckband. Pick up the stitches along the neck edge, then work the neckband to twice the desired depth. Do not bind off the stitches, but fold the band to the wrong side and slip stitch the open stitches to the fabric.

How to Attach and Hem CONTINUED

Stitch by stitch on a hem

A finished stockinette stitch hem worked stitch by stitch, shown on the right side.

A finished stockinette stitch hem worked stitch by stitch, shown on the wrong side. Use an open cast-on for the hem.

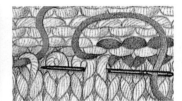

1 Graft the open cast-on stitches of the hem to the reverse stockinette side of the fabric, matching stitch for stitch.

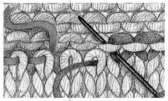

2 On the fabric, follow the line of the purl stitches.

Knitted-in band on the right-hand side

A knit one, purl one band worked along the slip stitch selvage of a stockinette stitch piece.

1 Cast on and *rib one row of the band to the last stitch (a knit stitch) leaving it on the left needle. Insert left needle under the first selvage stitch on the main piece and knit it together with the stitch on the left needle.

2 Turn the work and slip the first stitch purlwise with the yarn in the front, rib to the end. Repeat from the *.

Knitted-in band on the left-hand side

A knit one, purl one band worked along the slip stitch selvage of a stockinette stitch piece.

1 *Rib to last stitch of band (a purl stitch). With yarn in front, slip stitch purlwise, turn band. With yarn in back, insert left needle into first selvage stitch on main piece; knit it together with the slipped stitch.

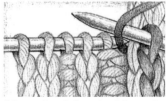

2 Leave the stitch on the right needle and rib to the end of the row. Repeat from the *.

VII. Design Details

SHORT ROW SHAPING

Short rows are partial rows of knitting that are used to shape or curve sections or to compensate for patterns with different row gauges. The result is that one side or section has more rows than the other, but no stitches are decreased. This technique is sometimes called turning because the work is turned within the row. Short rows can be worked on one or both sides of the piece at the same time.

Shaping with short rows eliminates the jagged edges that occur when you bind off a series of stitches such as at shoulders or on collars. After working short rows at a shoulder, bind off all the stitches at one time or join them to another piece directly from the needles.

When working with patterns of varying row gauges, short rows can be used to add rows to the shorter sections, allowing the finished piece to lie flat.

Short row shaping can also be used for darts, back necks on circular yokes, hats and medallions with circular pieces, and sock heels.

When you add an extra row into the knit piece, you must make a smooth transition between the edge where one row is worked and the edge that has the extra row. Do this by wrapping a slipped stitch, using one technique for knit stitches and another for purl stitches.

WRAPPING STITCHES (KNIT SIDE)

1 To prevent holes in the piece and create a smooth transition, wrap a knit stitch as follows: With the yarn in back, slip the next stitch purlwise.

2 Move the yarn between the needles to the front of the work.

3 Slip the same stitch back to the left needle. Turn the work, bringing the yarn to the purl side between the needles. One stitch is wrapped.

4 When you have completed all the short rows, you must hide the wraps. Work to just before the wrapped stitch. Insert the right needle under the wrap and knitwise into the wrapped stitch. Knit them together.

WRAPPING STITCHES (PURL SIDE)

1 To prevent holes in the piece and create a smooth transition, wrap a purl stitch as follows: With the yarn at the front, slip the next stitch purlwise.

2 Move the yarn between the needles to the back of the work.

3 Slip the same stitch back to the left needle. Turn the work, bringing the yarn back to the purl side between the needles. One stitch is wrapped.

4 After working the short rows, you must hide the wraps. Work to just before the wrapped stitch. Insert the right needle from behind into the back loop of the wrap. Place it on the left needle, as shown. Purl it together with the stitch on the left needle.

Selvages

The selvage (or selvedge) of knit fabric is an edge formed by changing the stitch pattern at the beginning and end of every row. This stabilizes the fabric and prepares it for seaming or creates a finished edge on pieces that will have no further finishing.

You can add selvage stitches to an existing pattern or when designing your own garments. Be sure to add them to the total stitch count. Usually a selvage is one stitch, but it can be two or more. Multiple-stitch selvages are most often used to prevent curling on non-seamed pieces, such as scarves.

Selvage stitches form a firm edge, which is helpful when working openwork patterns that tend to widen, or with slippery yarns, such as silk or rayon, which have a tendency to slide out of shape.

Selvage stitches can be used to avoid interrupting colorwork or stitch patterns with a seam. The selvage stitches serve as the seam allowance and disappear when the pieces are sewn.

Some selvages, such as garter or slip-stitch selvages, can help you keep track of rows. The knots or chains created on every other row make it easy to count the rows.

You should work all increases and decreases inside selvage edges, but when you shape a piece by binding off stitches, the selvage stitch will also disappear. Establish it again on the first row that is worked even. Always measure inside selvage edges.

One-Stitch Selvages

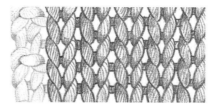

Garter stitch selvage (left side) This selvage is best worked on stockinette stitch fabrics and is the easiest selvage for beginners.

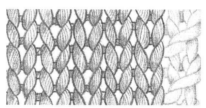

Garter stitch selvage (right side) The selvage looks slightly different on the right edge, as shown here. Work left and right edges as follows: *Row 1:* Knit one, work to the last stitch, knit one. Repeat this row.

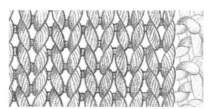

Reverse stockinette stitch selvage Suitable for stockinette stitch, this is easy for beginners. Work both sides as follows: *Row 1 (right side):* Purl one, work to the last stitch, purl one. *Row 2:* Knit one, work to the last stitch, knit one. Repeat these two rows.

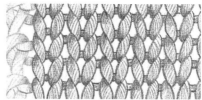

Slip garter stitch selvage (left side) This selvage is similar to the garter stitch selvage, only firmer. It is ideal for patterns that tend to spread laterally. The left side shown above is slightly different than the right side.

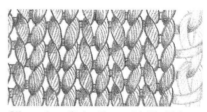

Slip garter stitch selvage (right side) Work both sides of the slip garter stitch selvage as follows: *Row 1:* Slip the first stitch knitwise, work to the last stitch, knit one. Repeat this row.

Chain stitch selvage This selvage is for garter stitch and is worked as follows: *Row 1:* With the yarn in front, slip the first stitch purlwise, with the yarn in back, knit to the end. Repeat this row.

SELVAGES CONTINUED

SLIP-STITCH SELVAGES

This method has three variations. All of them make a chain stitch edge, with each chain loop representing two rows. It is perfect to use when you must later pick up stitches.

English method *Row 1 (right side):* Slip the first stitch knitwise, work to the last stitch, slip the last stitch knitwise. *Row 2:* Purl one, work to the last stitch, purl one. Repeat these two rows.

French method *Row 1 (right side):* Slip the first stitch knitwise, work to the last stitch, knit one. *Row 2:* Slip the first stitch purlwise, work to the last stitch, purl one. Repeat these two rows.

German method *Row 1 (right side):* Knit the first stitch, work to the last stitch. With the yarn in back, slip the last stitch purlwise. *Row 2:* Purl the first stitch, work to the last stitch. With the yarn in front, slip the last stitch purlwise. Repeat these two rows.

TWO-STITCH SELVAGES

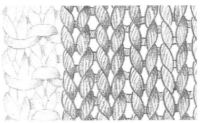

Double garter stitch selvage This is ideal for free-standing edges, such as scarves, and is worked as follows: *Row 1:* Slip the first stitch knitwise through the back loop, knit the second stitch, work to the last two stitches, knit two. Repeat this row.

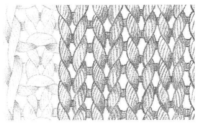

Chain garter stitch selvage This selvage is good for patterns with more depth, such as double knits.

Work the chain garter stitch selvage as follows: *Row 1 (right side):* With the yarn in back, slip the first stitch knitwise. With the yarn in front, purl the next stitch. Work to the last two stitches, purl the next stitch, slip the last stitch knitwise with the yarn in back. *Row 2:* Purl two, work to the last two stitches, purl two. Repeat these two rows.

DECORATIVE SELVAGES

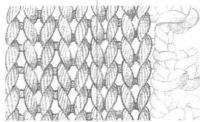

Beaded picot selvage Work this decorative alternative to a simple selvage as follows: *Row 1:* Cast on two or three stitches (as desired). Bind off these stitches, work to the end. On the next row, repeat row 1. Repeat these two rows as desired.

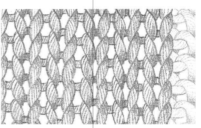

Picot selvage This makes a dainty trim on baby garments and shawls. It can also be used as a button loop for small buttons.

The picot selvage is worked as follows: *Row 1 (right side):* Bring the yarn over the right needle to the back and knit the first two stitches together. Work to the last two stitches, slip these two stitches knitwise, and pass the first stitch over the second stitch. *Row 2:* Bring the yarn over the right needle from front to back and to the front again and purl two, work to the last two stitches, purl two. Repeat these two rows.

PLACKETS

Plackets are used to create an opening for the neck at the front, at the back, or on a shoulder edge. Usually the placket border is worked and then the collar or neckband is added. Collars can be worked to the edges of the placket or to the center so that the collar meets when the buttons are closed.

Plan the depth and width of a placket to fit into the overall design. With a center cable pattern, the placket can be the width of that center cable. A long placket can create the illusion of a mock cardigan. A wide placket can be made with two rows of buttonholes for a double-breasted effect. A narrow, short placket is ideal for children's or baby garments.

As with other types of ribbed bands, plackets are usually worked on smaller needles, and care should be taken to pick up the correct number of stitches and to work to the correct length. Too many or too few stitches or rows will result in a placket that doesn't lie flat.

The button-band side of the placket is usually worked first. Mark the placement of the buttons on the button band and then work the buttonhole side. Overlap the plackets with the button band under the buttonhole band. The lower edge should be sewn neatly so that the placket doesn't bunch or buckle.

VERTICAL PLACKETS

Ribbed placket: horizontal A placket can be worked as shown by picking up stitches along the side edges and working to the depth of the placket width. Bind off evenly for a neat edge.

Ribbed placket: vertical This is worked by picking up stitches along the lower edge of the placket. Sew the side edges once the band is complete.

Making a vertical placket To work a vertical ribbed placket, leave the stitches on a holder until the piece is complete. Work the button band by picking up stitches behind the stitches on the holder. Work the buttonhole band directly from the holder stitches.

HORIZONTAL PLACKETS

When working a horizontal placket along the shoulder, make the left armhole depth shorter to accommodate the depth of the picked-up placket on the front and back pieces. You can work the ribbing along with the piece. Work the neckband once the placket is complete.

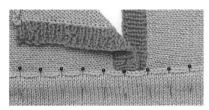

To sew the sleeve onto the horizontal placket, overlap the placket, pin the sleeve, and sew it in place through both layers of the overlapped placket.

BUTTONHOLES

Many different types of buttonholes include horizontal, vertical, eyelet, button loops, and those made from contrasting thread. You can also use the yarn overs of lace stitch patterns as buttonholes. Such a yarn-over buttonhole will need to be reinforced by overcasting after it is completed. You can also make buttonholes on loose knits by simply slipping the button through the stitch. (This type of buttonhole must also be reinforced.)

Which buttonhole you use will depend on the type of garment, how it will be worn, the position of the buttonhole, the size and type of button, and your yarn. For example, a coat with large buttons that is frequently buttoned will need large, durable buttonholes, and heavier yarn will make a larger buttonhole than finer yarn over the same number of stitches.

If possible, buy your buttons before making the buttonholes. Make a sample swatch with buttonholes to determine whether your buttons are the correct size. The buttonhole should be just large enough to slip the button through it. Since the knitted fabric stretches, a buttonhole that is too large will eventually cause buttons to unfasten. The buttonhole for a flat button must be smaller than that for a raised button of the same diameter.

Mark button placement on the appropriate band with contrasting yarn or safety pins before you work the buttonholes. On the opposite band, work the buttonholes to correspond to the button markers. Buttons are usually placed on the left side for women and the right side for men. Make sure that you use enough buttons to prevent the band from gapping.

Horizontal buttonholes should always be centered on bands. On vertical bands, try to have at least two stitches on either side of the buttonhole to prevent the buttonhole from stretching out. On horizontal bands, work the buttonholes when you have completed one-half the band.

You must work two identical buttonholes on foldover bands so that they will align when the band is folded.

To stabilize the buttonhole area when you use silk or rayon yarns, add a matching sewing thread when you work the buttonhole.

When making buttonholes, remember that when you bind off stitches, you must offset them by casting on (usually on the next row). Yarn overs must be offset by decreases. You usually work the first row of a buttonhole on the right side of the piece unless otherwise stated.

Perfect buttonholes take practice, so try a few before actually making them on your garment.

TWO-ROW HORIZONTAL BUTTONHOLES

The two-row buttonhole is made by binding off a number of stitches on one row and casting them on again on the next. The last stitch bound off is part of the left side of the buttonhole. The single cast-on makes the neatest edge for the upper part of the buttonhole. Some versions have techniques to strengthen the corners. All the horizontal buttonholes shown below are worked over four stitches.

Simple two-row buttonhole This buttonhole is frequently used in knitting instructions.

1 On the first row, work to the placement of the buttonhole. Knit two, with the left needle, pull one stitch over the other stitch, *knit one, pull the second stitch over the knit one; repeat from the * twice more. Four stitches have been bound off.

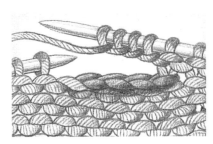

2 On the next row, work to the bound-off stitches and cast on four stitches using the single cast-on method. On the next row, work these stitches through the back loops to tighten them.

Version A *Row 1:* Work as for simple two-row. *Row 2:* Work to within one stitch of the bound-off stitches, increase one stitch (work into front and back of stitch), then cast on three stitches (the bound-off stitches less one) with the single cast-on method.

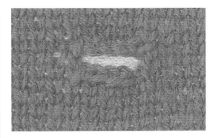

Version B *Row 1:* Bind off three stitches. Slip the last one to left needle, knit it together with the next stitch. *Row 2:* At the bound-off stitches, cast on five stitches. *Row 3:* Work to one stitch before the extra cast-on stitch, knit two together.

Version C *Row 1:* Work as for simple two-row. *Row 2:* At bound-off stitches, cast on four stitches, insert right needle from back to front under both loops of first bound-off stitch leaving loops on needle, work to end. *Row 3:* Knit bound-off loops with last cast-on stitch.

BUTTONHOLES CONTINUED

ONE-ROW HORIZONTAL BUTTONHOLE

The horizontal one-row buttonhole is the neatest buttonhole and requires no further reinforcing. It is shown here worked from the right side (lower buttonhole) and from the wrong side (upper buttonhole).

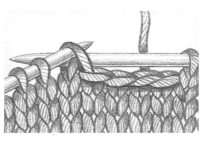

1 Work to the buttonhole, bring yarn to front, and slip a stitch purlwise. Place yarn at back and leave it there. *Slip next stitch from left needle. Pass the first slipped stitch over it; repeat from the * three times more (not moving yarn). Slip the last bound-off stitch to left needle and turn work.

2 Using the cable cast-on with the yarn at the back, cast on five stitches as follows: *Insert the right needle between the first and second stitches on the left needle, draw up a loop, place the loop on the left needle; repeat from the * four times more, turn the work.

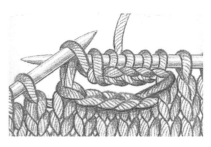

3 Slip the first stitch with the yarn in back from the left needle and pass the extra cast-on stitch over it to close the buttonhole. Work to the end of the row.

VERTICAL BUTTONHOLES

Vertical buttonhole slits are made by working two sections with separate balls of yarn at the same time or individually. If the latter, work the first side to desired depth (end at buttonhole edge). Work second side with one row less ending on wrong side. Turn work, cut second ball of yarn. Then, with yarn from first side, rejoin by working across all stitches.

Finish and strengthen by making a horizontal stitch at upper and lower joining points (use yarn from joining).

Seed stitch Vertical buttonholes can be worked on narrow bands. This type of buttonhole is not suited for large buttons or stress, and is best used for decorative purposes, such as on pocket flaps. Seed stitch is ideal for vertical buttonholes since it lies flat.

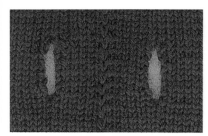

Double buttonholes Since stockinette stitch rolls inward, vertical buttonholes should only be used on stockinette stitch for double bands as shown here. To make a neater edge, add a selvage stitch on either side of the slit.

Closed double buttonholes When the band is complete, fold it, match the buttonholes, and reinforce them by embroidering with the buttonhole stitch. Note that the band is worked with a slip stitch at the center to make a neater folding edge.

CONTRASTING YARN BUTTONHOLE

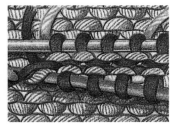

Another buttonhole method is to work the buttonhole stitches with a short piece of contrasting yarn. Then slip the stitches back to the left needle and reknit them with the main-color yarn. Leave the contrasting yarn in the buttonhole.

1 From the back of the work, using the main color and a crochet hook, pull through a loop in each stitch on the lower edge of the buttonhole and pick up one stitch from the side edge. Slip these five loops from the hook to a cable needle.

2 Working along the top edge, pick up four loops and one from the side. Transfer the five loops to a cable or double-pointed needle. Cut the yarn, leaving a strand about eight inches (20cm) long.

3 Fasten down each loop to the fabric with a yarn needle. Remove the contrasting yarn. Use this method when you add a ribbon band for reinforcement. Cut the space for the buttonhole on the ribbon before you pick up the loops and anchor them over the ribbon.

EYELET BUTTONHOLES

One-stitch eyelet: version A Eyelet buttonholes are small and are ideal for small buttons and children's garments. Work as follows: *Row 1:* Work to the buttonhole, knit two together, yarn over. *Row 2:* Work the yarn over as a stitch on next row.

One-stitch eyelet: version B *Row 1:* Work to the buttonhole, yarn over. *Row 2:* Slip yarn over, then yarn over again. *Row 3:* Slip one stitch knitwise before yarn overs, knit them together, leaving them on left needle. Pass slip stitch over the stitch just made. Knit yarn overs together with the next stitch on needle.

Two-stitch eyelet: version A *Row 1:* Work to the buttonhole, knit two together, yarn over twice, slip, slip, knit (ssk). *Row 2:* Work the yarn overs as follows: Purl into the first yarn over and then purl into the back of the second yarn over.

Two-stitch eyelet: version B *Row 1:* Work to the buttonhole, yarn over twice, knit two together through back loops. *Row 2:* Work to the yarn overs, purl the first yarn over and drop the second yarn over from the needle.

BUTTONHOLES CONTINUED

OVERCAST BUTTON LOOP

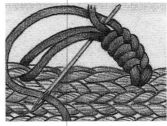

Button loops are worked after the piece is complete and are generally used where only one or two buttons are needed. Loops are ideal for plackets in fine yarns, baby garments, or closures on jackets or coats.

1 Mark placement for the beginning and ending points of the loop on the side edge. To form the core of the loop, using a yarn needle and yarn, bring the needle up at the lower edge. Insert the needle at the upper marker. Pull the yarn through, leaving a loop the desired size.

2 Make a double strand by bringing the needle up at the lower marker once more. Depending on the size of the loop, this can be done once more to make a three-strand core.

3 Work the buttonhole stitch over all the loops by bringing the yarn to the left of the needle. Then insert the needle under the loops and over the yarn, pull the yarn through, and tighten.

CROCHETED BUTTON LOOP

You can easily adjust the size of this loop to the size of the button. The button loop should be just large enough to allow the button to pass through. If the loop is too large, the button will not stay securely.

1 Mark the placement as for the overcast button loop. With a crochet hook, pull up a loop at the upper marker and work a crochet chain to the desired length.

2 Remove the hook from the loop and insert it through the fabric at the lower marker, then through the last loop of the chain. Draw the loop through the fabric. Catch the yarn and pull it through the loop on the hook.

3 To work a row of single crochet over the chain, insert the hook under the chain and pull up a loop. Catch a strand of yarn with the hook and pull it through both loops on the hook. Fasten off the last loop and weave in ends.

FINISHING BUTTONHOLES

Sometimes even the best button-holes need a bit of reinforcing. How you do so will depend on the yarn and the size of the buttonhole. The buttonhole stitch shown is good for both single and double button-holes.

Buttonhole stitch Use either a whole or split strand of yarn with this reinforcing technique. Work from right to left around the button-hole, with the needle pointing toward the center. Don't work the stitches too closely or you may distort the buttonhole.

The overcasting method is good for simple eyelets used to make small buttonholes.

Overcasting This reinforcing technique is worked by overcasting evenly around the buttonhole.

BANDS, BORDERS, AND EDGES

Bands, borders, and edges are used to complete garments and to cover and flatten raw edges on knit pieces that have a tendency to curl. Bands and borders are usually wider than edges; they are used to give stability to pieces. Edges, such as those in lace patterns, are often used to add a decorative touch.

The classic ribbing stitch is often used for bands, but you can use a number of other stitch patterns. Choose those that don't curl, such as garter or seed stitch, except when curling is desired or for folded bands.

You can work a band at the same time as the piece, but for a firmer edge, work it separately on smaller needles. You can either pick up stitches to work a separate band or apply the band once the piece is complete. Prepare pieces for picked-up bands by adding selvage stitches on the edges. For picked-up bands, be sure to have the correct number of stitches. Too few stitches will make the band pull in; too many will cause it to wobble or ruffle. Check the band gauge on your knit swatch.

You can make bands and borders of single or double thickness. They are usually not more than an inch or two (2.5cm or 5cm) wide, so that they remain stable. Bands can also be reinforced with ribbon or tape to keep them firm.

RIBBED BANDS

Ribbed bands are flexible and elastic, which makes them perfect for areas that are intended to grip. They can be simple knit one, purl one or knit two, purl two ribbing or some of the other variations shown below.

Horizontal This band, more elastic than a vertical one, is often used on cardigan or jacket fronts. It is the easiest type of band to work, but it requires careful attention to make sure that you pick up the correct number of stitches for an even, flat edge.

Vertical For an unbroken line, you can work vertical bands from ribbing stitches left on a holder after the lower edge is complete. Once beginning the band, add a selvage stitch for seaming.

To attach the vertical band, pin it along the edge as you work, without stretching it. Then either bind off the stitches or leave them on a holder to work the neckband. Sew the band in place.

Purl three, knit one ribbing (a multiple of four stitches plus three extra) *Row 1 (right side):* *Purl three, knit one; repeat from the *, end purl three. *Row 2:* *Knit three, purl one; repeat from the *, end knit three. Repeat these two rows.

Stockinette/garter stitch ribbing (a multiple of four stitches plus two extra) *Row 1 (right side):* Knit. *Row 2:* *Purl two, knit two; repeat from the *, end purl two. Repeat these two rows.

Stockinette/seed stitch ribbing (a multiple of four stitches plus two extra) *Row 1 (right side):* *Knit two, purl one, knit one; repeat from the *, end knit two. *Row 2:* *Purl two, knit one, purl one; repeat from the *, end purl two. Repeat these two rows.

STOCKINETTE STITCH BANDS

Doubled on a curve This band is picked up and worked with a turning ridge. To keep the curved edges flat, decrease stitches on every knit row up to the turning ridge, then increase to correspond on the second half.

Picot band Pick up an odd number of stitches for this doubled band. Work picot row on the right side as follows: *Knit two together, yarn over; repeat from the *, end knit one. Work inside band to match outside.

Bias band This band is worked separately and then sewn onto the piece. Increase one stitch at the beginning of each right-side row and decrease one stitch at the end of the same row.

Outside rolled band Pick up stitches from right side edge. Beginning with a purl row, work in stockinette stitch for four or five rows. Bind off. The purl side rolls to outside.

Inside rolled band Pick up stitches from right side edge. Beginning with a knit row, work in stockinette stitch for four or five rows. Bind off. The purl side rolls to inside.

BANDS, BORDERS, AND EDGES CONTINUED

KNIT-IN BORDERS

The advantage of knit-in borders is that your piece is complete once you have finished the knitting. The best stitches are those that lie flat, such as ribbing, seed stitch, or the bias edge shown here. Avoid working stitches that may differ in row gauge from your piece, such as stockinette with garter stitch. When working bands in contrasting colors, twist yarns on the wrong side to prevent holes.

GARTER STITCH BORDERS WITH CORNERS

These borders, ideal for jackets, shawls, or blankets, are worked separately. Since corners are wider at the outer edge, you make decreases on either side of a central stitch at each corner. To determine the number of stitches to cast on, measure all side edges and multiply this number by the stitch gauge. Then find required number of decreases by multiplying band width by row gauge. Add the number of decreases (for each corner) to find the number of stitches to be cast on.

Ribbing on a curve To shape an armhole and make the band at the same time, rib two stitches, then decrease one stitch. On right-side rows, keep increasing one stitch at the edge (in rib) and decreasing inside the ribbing edge until the armhole is shaped and the desired stitches are in the rib pattern.

Seed stitch This is a good choice for a border on a stockinette stitch body, since it has the same row gauge as stockinette stitch. Also, a seed stitch pattern makes a nice flat edge.

Bias Leave this stockinette stitch band flat or fold it in half to the inside and sew it in place. On right-side rows, slip the first stitch knitwise, work a make one increase, work to the last two stitches of the band, knit two together. On wrong-side rows, purl all border stitches.

Knit corner Cast on and mark each corner. Knit to two stitches before the corner, knit two together, knit the corner stitch, knit two together through the back loops. On wrong-side rows, purl the corner stitches and knit the remaining stitches.

Eyelet corner Cast on and mark each corner. Work to three stitches before the corner, knit three together, yarn over, knit the corner stitch, yarn over, knit three together through the back loops. On wrong-side rows, purl the corner stitch and knit all the others.

MISCELLANEOUS BANDS

Garter stitch band Work this band by picking up two stitches for every three rows along a straight edge. Knit every row. Bind off.

Pick up and knit border This border makes a good, firm, narrow edge and is sometimes called "mock crochet." Pick up the stitches and then bind them off on the next row. Or knit one row and then bind off.

Held miter band Cast on stitches to desired width, plus width of band. Work one stitch less on each row, placing it on a holder. When reaching the desired band depth, work the piece, leaving the stitches on a holder for the mitered edge.

Pick up stitches along the side edge. On right-side rows, knit a band stitch with a holder stitch, then work a make one increase. On wrong-side rows, work to the last stitch, make one, work the last stitch together with the next holder stitch.

Open chain cast-on

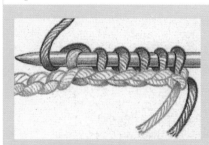

1 Use this cast-on to later add a band. Chain the number of stitches above the rib in contrasting yarn. With main-color yarn, pick up one stitch in the back loop of each chain.

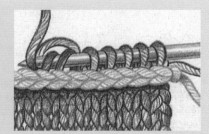

2 After the piece is complete, to work band with a smaller needle, pick up the main-color loops under the chain, working two loops together, as shown, if decreasing is desired.

3 When the band is complete, remove the chain from the piece.

CROCHET EDGES

SINGLE CROCHET

One row of single crochet, shown above, makes a neat, narrow edge; several rows form a firm edge. You can also use it as a base for other crochet edges.

Single crochet can be worked on a slip stitch base, as shown here.

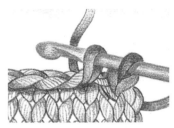

1 Draw through a loop as for a slip stitch, bring the yarn over the hook, and pull it through the first loop. *Insert the hook into the next stitch and draw through a second loop.

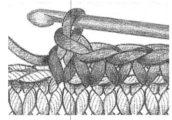

2 Yarn over and pull through both loops on the hook. Repeat from the * to the end.

BACKWARD SINGLE CROCHET (CRAB STITCH)

Work a backward single crochet edge the same as a single crochet, but from left to right rather than right to left.

This edge, a variation of the simple backward single crochet, is worked by making a backward single crochet in one stitch, making a chain one, and skipping a stitch.

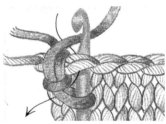

1 Pull through a loop on the left edge. Chain one. *Go into the next stitch to the right. Catch the yarn as shown and pull it through the fabric, then underneath (not through) the loop on the hook.

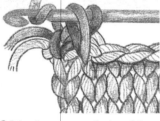

2 Bring the yarn over the top of the crochet hook and around as shown, then draw the yarn through both loops. Repeat from the *.

Hems

A hem or facing is an edge that folds under to keep the knitting from curling or stretching. It is usually made to replace ribbing and can be made horizontally or vertically. It allows pieces to hang properly and is ideal for edges that do not hug the body. Hems can be used for lower edges of knit garments or necklines and front edges of cardigans and coats.

A hem can also be used to form a casing for elastic, such as at the top of a skirt. It can be worked at the same time as the piece or picked up after it is complete.

The edge of the hem can be distinct (turning ridge) or rounded (without turning ridge). The folded part of the hem should be made in a smooth stitch such as stockinette, regardless of the stitch pattern used for the piece, and should be worked on a needle at least one size smaller—possibly even two or three sizes smaller—than the needles used for the main body. You may have to increase or decrease stitches once the hem is complete, depending on the gauge of the stitch pattern above the hem. Try a small sample before you begin. Hems are not ideal to use with openwork patterns, since the folded area will show through.

The folded edge should be sewn to the garment as invisibly as possible with whip stitch or blind stitch, or sewn stitch by stitch from the knitting needle.

Turning ridges

A turning ridge is used to create a clean line that makes a neat edge when the hem is sewn in place. All ridges are made after the hem is the desired depth, whether they are at the lower or the upper edge. The piece worked before (at the lower edge) or after (at the upper edge) is the hem.

Purl A ridge is formed by knitting the stitches through the back loops on the wrong side, thus forming a purl ridge on the right side of the work. On the following (right-side) row, begin the body pattern.

Picot This ridge is worked over an even number of stitches. Work the picot row on the right side as follows: Knit one stitch, *knit two stitches together, yarn over; repeat from the *, ending with a knit one.

Slip stitch This turning ridge is worked over an odd number of stitches. Work the slip stitch row on the right side as follows: *Knit one. With the yarn at the front, slip one stitch, knit one; repeat from the * to the end.

HEMS CONTINUED

KNIT-IN HEM

To reduce bulk, the cast-on edge is worked together with stitches on the needle so that sewing is not necessary.

This knit-in hem was worked using a regular cast-on. Stitches were picked up along the cast-on row and placed on a spare needle. It should be noted that a knit-in hem is not easy to unravel if corrections must be made.

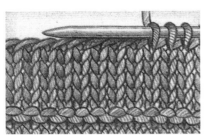

1 Work the hem to the desired depth and then make a turning ridge. Work the main piece until it is the same depth as the hem, end with a wrong-side row. Using a spare needle and separate yarn, pick up one loop from the cast-on edge for each stitch on the main needle.

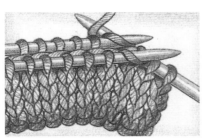

2 Cut the extra yarn. Then fold up the hem and knit one stitch from the spare needle together with one stitch from the main piece as shown. Continue in pattern, beginning with a wrong-side row.

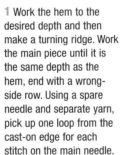

VERTICAL FACINGS

Vertical facings can be worked at the same time the garment is made or picked up and worked later. These facings are ideal for a tailored jacket and cardigan fronts. When the facing is to be picked up later, make a selvage stitch at the edge to aid in the pick-up. Steam or wet block the pieces carefully before stitching the facing in place.

Garter stitch A simple facing can be made by using a garter stitch as a turning ridge. On every row, knit the turning ridge stitch.

Slip stitch For a cardigan front, a band can be worked with double buttonholes. Work the slip stitch turning ridge by slipping the stitch purlwise on right-side rows and purling it on wrong-side rows. Fold the band and reinforce the buttonholes through both thicknesses.

Picked-up After the piece is worked, pick up three stitches for every four along the edge and work the desired depth. Stitches can be bound off as shown or sewn down stitch by stitch.

Mitered facing and hem

When making a garment with a horizontal hem and vertical facing, you can reduce bulk and create a smooth edge by making edges that meet but don't overlap. To do this, calculate the number of rows in the hem depth. Divide this in half and reduce the number of stitches you cast on by the result (about one inch/2.5cm).

After casting on, work the hem by increasing one stitch every other row until all the stitches are added back. Make a turning ridge. For the front facing, increase one stitch every other row, adding one stitch for the front turning ridge.

On this mitered edge, increase one stitch every other row four times before making the purl turning ridge, then make the facing by increasing one stitch every other row plus one stitch for the garter stitch turning ridge. Sew the hem and facing, carefully matching the corners.

Pockets

Generally, pockets are worked in unshaped areas of a garment so as not to interrupt its design. The most common types are patch, horizontal inset, and vertical inset. Pockets should be in proportion to your garment. For example, don't make a tiny pocket opening on a bulky jacket.

The average size of a woman's pocket is five to six-and-a-half inches (12.5 to 16.5cm) wide by five-and-a-half to seven inches (14 to 17.5cm) deep. For a man's pocket, add an inch (2.5cm), and for a child's pocket, subtract an inch (2.5cm) or more.

Place the pocket at a level that is comfortable for your hands. The easiest way is to check an existing sweater.

On a woman's sweater, the lower edge of a horizontal or patch pocket should be no farther than 21 or 22 inches (53 or 56cm) from the shoulder and approximately two-and-a-half to four inches (6.5 to 10cm) from the center front edge. Vertical or side seam pockets are easier to wear in cropped sweaters.

If you want to add pockets to a garment, you will need to decide what type of pocket and edging, where to place the pocket, and whether it should contrast or match your sweater's yarn and pattern. Work with the stitch and row gauge of your design to calculate the number of stitches and rows needed for the pocket. Don't forget to add a little extra yarn to the amount required for the garment.

Patch pockets

Simple square or rectangular patch pockets are easiest to make. You can also work patch pockets in contrasting stitch patterns, colors, or other shapes, such as circles or triangles.

It is essential to work neatly. Apply the pocket subtly with a nearly invisible stitch or boldly using a contrasting color in blanket stitch. Pockets in non-curling stitches, such as garter or seed stitch are easiest to apply. For a neater edge, add a slip stitch selvage to side edges.

Simple pocket Patch pockets should be applied to firmly knit pieces in stable yarns that can support the extra weight of the pocket. For easier application, place the pocket directly above the rib or hem. This gives you a straight line along the lower edge.

Simple with a cable A patch pocket can be made with a center cable that goes over the body cable. Line up the pocket cable over the body cable and sew in place.

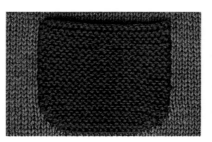

Curved lower edge For this pocket, cast on the desired number of stitches, less four to six depending on the pocket size and yarn. *Work one row even. Cast on one stitch at each end of the next row. Repeat from the * to add back the four to six stitches.

Applying a patch pocket

Block or press the pocket. Measure it and outline an area the same size on the garment, using a contrasting yarn in the basting stitch. Pin the pocket over the area before applying. Then overcast the pocket in place.

An alternate method of applying a patch pocket is to run a needle in and out of one-half of every other row along both vertical edges of the pocket and one-half of every stitch along the lower edge of the pocket.

Pin the pocket in place in the center of the needles and, using the overcast stitch, sew one stitch from the needle and one stitch from the pocket.

To make a neater, nearly invisible pocket seam, use duplicate stitch along the edges through the pocket and the body piece as shown.

Patch pockets with hemmed edges

The hemmed patch pocket has folded lower and side edges. Cast on the desired number of stitches and work tightly in stockinette stitch for approximately one-half inch (1.5cm), depending on the weight of the yarn (heavier yarn may need more depth).

1 Work a turning ridge by knitting one row through the back loops on the purl (wrong) side. Work the same depth above the turning ridge. Cast on two to four stitches at the beginning and end for side hems.

2 Continue to work pocket, slipping the first stitch inside of the side hems on right-side rows and purling this stitch on wrong-side rows. Work to the desired length.

3 Add a ribbed edge (about one-half to one inch/1.5 to 2.5cm) or work another turning ridge at the top of the pocket and fold the edge under. Bind off all stitches. Backstitch the lower edge as shown, then flip the pocket up and whip stitch the two side edges.

POCKETS CONTINUED

PICKED-UP PATCH POCKETS

This patch pocket looks like a set-in pocket. You can knit the pocket as a flap and then sew it in place, or you can pick up the side edges and apply it as you knit.

1 If desired, baste a line along the desired placement line of the pocket. With a crochet hook, pick up one stitch for each stitch of the pocket, placing the stitches on a knitting needle. Work one row even on the wrong side.

2 To attach at the right edge, skip one row on the piece. With the right needle, pick up one-half of the stitch in the next row (directly over the first stitch of the pocket), slip it to the left needle, and knit it together with the first stitch of the pocket.

3 To attach at the left edge, slip the last stitch knitwise to the right needle and with the left needle, pick up one-half of the stitch on the piece, slip the stitch back to the left needle and knit it together with the picked-up stitch through the back loops as shown.

POCKET FLAPS

Pocket flaps can be picked up and knit or made separately and sewn on. The flap should be the width of the pocket. Apply the flap slightly above the pocket opening.

You can attach flaps as you knit by working the flap first and leaving the stitches on a holder. Then knit together a stitch of the flap and one of the piece.

Rectangle This pocket flap can be made with or without a border. It can also be used without a pocket to create the look of a mock pocket.

Triangle This pocket flap is made with a buttonhole. The buttonhole can be vertical or horizontal and can be decorative or functional.

Outside flap When the pocket is the desired depth, you can make a flap on the outside of the pocket. First make a turning ridge and then work the flap by reversing the stitch pattern so that wrong-side rows become right-side rows.

INSET POCKETS

Inset pockets, the most common type, are inconspicuous. They can be made with a horizontal, vertical, or slanted opening. Although the ways to make this pocket vary, they all have the same basic elements.

The lining of the inset pocket is usually made before the piece is begun. (Information on making linings appears on page 103.)

Inset pockets can be made with a knit-in border or with one added later, which is usually three-fourths to one-and-a-half inches (2 to 4cm). A disadvantage of the knit-in border is that it may be too loose if the needle is the same size as the body. To make an added border, you can bind off the stitches or place them on a holder until you are ready to work the edge. To create a firmer edge on a ribbing border, bind off all the stitches knitwise.

HORIZONTAL INSET POCKETS: VERSION A

The horizontal inset pocket is one of the most frequently used methods for adding a pocket. You must first make a pocket lining, which is usually attached from the wrong side of the work.

2 On the next row, work the lining over the place where the stitches were bound off. For a neater join, add two extra stitches to the lining and work them together with the first and last stitches of the piece.

1 On the right side, work to the pocket placement and bind off to prepare for adding the pocket lining. The pocket edge is worked after the piece is complete.

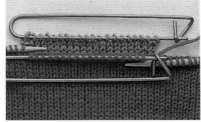

2a An alternate method of joining the lining in one row is to place the stitches on a holder. With the right side of the lining facing the wrong side of the piece, work the stitches of the lining, then work to the end of the row.

INSET POCKETS CONTINUED

HORIZONTAL INSET POCKETS: VERSION B

This inset pocket has an attached double lining that is worked in a strip and rejoined to the piece. The sides of the pocket are sewn later and the pocket lining hangs free.

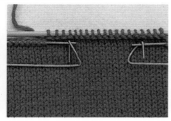

1 To begin this horizontal pocket on the right side, work to the pocket opening, place these stitches on a holder. Purl across stitches for the opening to make a turning ridge and place the remaining stitches on a holder.

2 Continue in stockinette stitch on the pocket lining for about eight inches (20cm), ending with a knit row. Fold the pocket lining in half and work the stitches from the second holder to the end of the row.

3 To rejoin the lining to the body, work to the pocket lining on the next row. Work across the stitches of the pocket lining. Slip the remaining stitches to a knitting needle and work to the end of the row. Sew the sides of the pocket lining.

VERTICAL INSET POCKETS: VERSION A

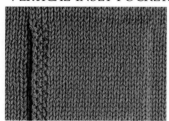

The vertical inset pocket on the right-hand side of the piece is made with a knit-in seed stitch border and an attached lining, or a lining flap for attaching a fabric or knit lining. Reverse the process for a left-side pocket.

1 On the right side of the piece, work to the pocket opening and place the remaining stitches on a holder. Continue to the desired depth, working a seed-stitch border at the pocket edge, ending with a wrong-side row. Place these stitches on a holder.

2 At the first holder, work the lining (or lining flap) by joining a second ball of yarn and casting on the additional stitches. It is shown here after a few rows have been worked. Work these stitches to the same depth as the first half of the pocket.

3 To rejoin the pocket, work to the pocket lining, then knit the lining stitches together with the stitches on the holder. Work to the end of the row. Continue in pattern.

Vertical inset pockets: version B

This vertical inset pocket is made by working a few rows of the pocket lining on separate needles, ending with a right-side row. Shown above is a pocket on the right-hand side of the piece. Reverse the process to make a pocket on the left-hand side.

1 Work to the edge of the pocket and place these stitches on a holder. Work to the end of the row. On the next row, work to the pocket edge, then work across the lining stitches. Work to the desired depth. Place these stitches on a holder.

2 Return to the stitches on the first holder and work to the depth of the lining stitches, ending with a wrong-side row. On the next row, work across all stitches (working the lining stitches together with the pocket stitches).

3 To work an edge along the vertical opening, pick up stitches along the pocket opening. After working the edging, sew down the side edges. Sew the lining to the wrong side.

Slanted/diagonal inset pockets

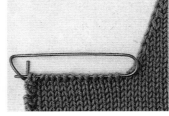

To make a slanted or diagonal pocket on the right-hand side of the piece, as shown above, you must know the desired depth, width, and angle of the pocket. A slanted pouch pocket can be made with two openings slanting in opposite directions on either side.

1 Work to the pocket opening and place the remaining stitches on a holder. Work the stitches, making decreases at the pocket opening edge as planned. Work to the desired depth and place these stitches on a second holder, ending with a wrong-side row.

2 Slip the stitches from first holder to a needle. With a second ball of yarn, cast on stitches for the lining equal to the total number of stitches in the pocket width. Work to the depth of the stitches on the second holder, ending with a wrong-side row.

3 Rejoin by working across all stitches (working lining stitches together with pocket stitches). An edge is added once the piece is complete. For a slanting edge, increase one stitch at the top of the opening and decrease one stitch at the lower edge on every other row.

Inset Pockets CONTINUED

SIDE-SEAM POCKETS

You can add a side-seam pocket on either side as an afterthought since it is worked once the pieces are complete.

Single A side-seam pocket can have a single pocket lining that is sewn to the wrong side of the front piece as shown. The lining can be a rectangle or a curve to fit the hand.

Double A side-seam pocket can also have a pocket lining that is worked double. It is sewn together and allowed to hang free after the top and bottom edges are sewn to the front and back of the piece.

Attached You can also work the lining at the same time as the piece, making identical linings on the front and the back, which are sewn together to create a double lining.

POUCH POCKETS

A pouch pocket can be made by making two vertical openings on either side of the front with one lining joining the two openings.

2 Work the desired pocket depth on all stitches. Place the stitches just worked on a holder. Work the stitches from the first holder to the same depth as the main piece, ending with a wrong-side row.

1 Work to the first pocket opening. Place the pocket stitches on a holder and leave at the front of the work. Cast onto the right needle the same number of stitches that you placed on the holder. Work to the end.

3 Join the pocket stitches to the lining by working one stitch from the pocket together with one stitch from the lining. When the entire piece is complete, sew the lower edge of the lining to the front. Work an edging on each side of the pouch.

Cut-in pockets

You can add a pocket by snipping one thread and pulling out the desired number of stitches. Make this easier by working the desired number of stitches in a contrasting yarn while you are knitting the piece.

1 Work the desired number of stitches in a contrasting yarn. Slip these stitches back to the left needle and knit them once more with the main color.

2 Once the piece is complete, remove the contrasting strand. Place the stitches on the upper edge on a holder. Apply a border to the stitches on the lower edge.

3 Work the lining down from the upper edge stitches as shown. Then sew down the lining stitches and attach the sides of the border to the front of the piece.

Making a pocket lining

Linings are most often knit from the same yarn as the piece. Although it is called a lining, this piece is really a backing for the pocket.

You can make the lining with the exact number of stitches of the pocket or you can add a stitch to either side. Then work them together with the sweater piece or bind them off before you join the lining to the piece.

After you work the lining, block it, keeping the stitches on a holder until you are ready to join it to the piece.

Stockinette stitch is the flattest stitch for a lining. When your body pattern is not stockinettte, work a few rows of the stockinette lining in the same stitch as the body to keep continuity of pattern.

When you use a bulky yarn, you can make the lining with a lighter yarn or of fabric that is attached to a knit

flap approximately one-and-a-half to two inches (4 to 5cm) wide or deep. This keeps the lining from showing. When using lightweight yarn, use the heavier yarn for the last few rows that will show. Double-strand garments should have a single-strand lining.

The lining should not go below the ribbing, as it may stretch and hang below the sweater edge. The lining should be tightly knit.

When attaching the lining, pin it first to make sure that it lies completely flat. Carefully slip stitch the lining in place, being sure that the stitching doesn't show through on the front of the piece.

POCKET EDGES/BORDERS

Outside rolled An interesting variation to the usual ribbed border is this stockinette stitch border that rolls to the outside of the pocket.

Cable This is another alternative to simple bands. This cable strip was made separately and then sewn onto the pocket.

Picot hem A stockinette stitch hem can be used to edge a pocket. The one shown here has a picot edge with a bobble pattern below the picot turning ridge.

Tips for making pocket edges

- Pocket edges are often worked in the same stitch and with the same size needles as the sweater edges or ribbing.

- Other than ribbing, good stitches for edges or borders are garter stitch, seed stitch, or reverse stockinette stitch. Crocheted edges also make good pocket openings.

- Take care to pick up the correct number of stitches. Too few stitches will cause the pocket to pull in and too many will cause it to gap.

- The proper bind-off is essential. You can bind off stitches in ribbing or knitwise—depending on the border and how loose or tight you need the edge to be.

- The edging pattern should be centered so that the first and last stitches match on either end.

- Fasten corners of pockets securely, as these edges receive the most stress. Use a double strand of yarn to reinforce edges.

- To eliminate further seaming as you work the border, attach the first and last stitches of the piece in the same way as you work a picked-up patch pocket.

BUTTONS

Buttons can add a striking contrast to your garment, or they can blend in subtly with the knit fabric. You can also make perfectly matching crochet buttons, which are shown here.

The button should be appropriate to the yarn. For example, leather or stone buttons work best on tweedy, rugged yarns for outdoor garments, and fancy glass buttons are best suited to tailored or dressy styles.

Take along a yarn sample when you buy buttons to find a good match. If possible, purchase an extra button or two to replace any you may lose.

Match the size of your button carefully to the size of your buttonhole so that the button will fit properly.

Buttons that cannot be washed should always be removed before cleaning. When you purchase buttons, look for any special care instructions on the package.

CROCHET BUTTON WITH RING

This type of button is made with a small plastic ring about one-half inch (1.5cm) wide. **1** Leaving a six-inch (15cm) tail, make a slip knot and work single crochets tightly around the ring. Join the last single crochet to the first. Cut the yarn, leaving an eight-inch (20cm) strand and pull through the last loop. **2** Thread the eight-inch (20cm) strand through a yarn needle and pick up the outside loop from every other single crochet. Gather them together and pull the strand to the back. Tie this strand tightly to the other one and use it to sew on the button.

STUFFED CROCHET BUTTON

1 Make a slip knot and chain three. Slip stitch into the first chain to join. Work two single crochets into each of the three chains. Continue to increase until there are 12 single crochets. To decrease on the next round, work two single crochets together six times. Cut the yarn, leaving an eight-inch (20cm) strand. Stuff the button with matching yarn. **2** Work the second step as for the crochet button with ring.

Sewing on buttons

To sew on buttons, you can use yarn (if it goes through the button), matching thread, or pearl cotton. When sewing on metal buttons, which tend to cut the thread, you may wish to use waxed dental floss. Double the thread and tie a knot on the end. Then slip your button onto the needle and thread. You can further secure the button, which is especially desirable on garments that receive heavy wear, such as jackets. After going into the button and the fabric several times, wrap the thread around the button a few times and go back to the wrong side.

Add a small button or square of knitting or felt on the wrong side to keep the button in place.

Knotted thread has a tendency to pull through knit fabric. Lock it in place by inserting thread into

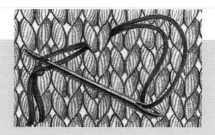

fabric on the right side and through the doubled thread. Clip knotted end.

FINISHING TOUCHES

The most important part of finishing is all the little details that don't show when the sweater is worn. Careful attention to these details can improve the look and fit of your knit garments.

Remember that knit fabric is not stable and must be treated somewhat differently than woven fabric. To help stabilize your knits, you can add seam binding to shoulder seams, ribbon facings to the front of cardigans, and linings to jackets and skirts.

As with woven pieces, you can add zippers to skirts and jackets and elastic waistbands to skirts. You can make matching buttons or attach purchased buttons in special ways to prevent the fabric from stretching.

Your finishing materials and the yarn for your garment should be compatible in their cleaning. If not, dry clean, or attach any notions so that you can remove them easily before cleaning.

RIBBON FACINGS

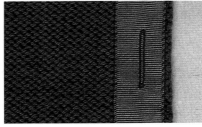

A ribbon facing is sewn in place and finished with machine-sewn buttonholes.

Ribbon facings, usually grosgrain ribbon, are generally sewn to the inside of the band, but decorative ribbon can also be used on the outside at the edges. On the button band, the ribbon helps support the button. On the buttonhole band, the ribbon adds stability to the buttonhole openings. You can knit in buttonholes and then cut matching openings in the ribbon and join the two edges with the buttonhole stitch. Or once the ribbon is in place, you can machine sew the buttonholes through the knitting and the ribbon and cut through both layers.

Wash and dry the ribbon before attaching to pre-shrink it. The ribbon should be applied to blocked pieces. Cut two pieces to fit along the front edges with a one-fourth inch (1cm) seam allowance on each end. Fold the seam allowance under and pin or baste the ribbon to the band. Pin the

center and work out to either side to make an even edge. With a matching sewing thread, sew the band in place, easing in the knitting. Work the buttonhole band first. After machine- or handsewing the buttonholes, check the length with the button-band side. Making buttonholes can shorten the buttonhole side slightly.

Taping a seam

A narrow twill tape or seam binding can be used along seams to prevent them from stretching. This can be done after seaming and is especially good for areas such as shoulders that may need to be stabilized. The tape can also be used to ease in a shoulder that is too wide.

Cut a piece of tape the length of the desired shoulder width and whip stitch the tape on either side along the shoulder seam, easing in the fullness as desired.

USING ELASTIC

Elastic waistbands are often used for knit skirts. The width of the elastic depends on the type of yarn and skirt you are making. In general, the most comfortable elastic for waist-bands is at least one inch (2.5cm) wide. Some elastic made especially for waistbands is thicker and stronger than regular elastic. Cut the elastic to fit the waist plus an inch (2.5cm) for overlapping.

For a hem casing, the raw edges of the elastic should be overlapped and sewn together after the elastic is inserted into the casing. For the herringbone method, overlap and sew the elastic edges before working the herringbone stitching.

The simplest waistband is a hem casing worked in a flat stitch with a turning ridge. When sewn, the casing must be deep enough to allow the elastic to move easily. Sew the casing with a slip stitch, leaving two inches (5cm) open to insert the elastic. Attach a safety pin to one end of the elastic and draw it through the casing, taking care not to twist it. You might wish to pin the other end of the elastic to the piece so it doesn't get drawn into the casing. Join the elastic and finish sewing the hem.

An alternate casing method is to use a long crocheted chain and slip stitch it in a zigzag over the elastic. This is slightly bulkier than the herringbone method, but less bulky than the hem casing method.

HERRINGBONE METHOD

The herringbone method makes a single thickness, which adds no bulk to the waist. When you are finished, the elastic should move freely and not be caught in the stitching. Use a strong thread that won't fray as the elastic moves.

The first step is to place four pins an equal distance apart around the joined elastic. Then place four pins an equal distance apart around the skirt. Pin the elastic to the waist of the skirt, matching the pins and stretching the elastic to fit.

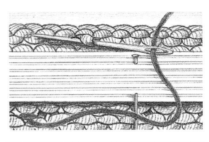

1 Use strong thread and a yarn needle. Working from left to right, secure the thread below the elastic. Insert the needle through one loop of the stitch that is three stitch-es to the right above the elastic.

2 Insert the needle down into the loop of the stitch that is three stitches to the right and below the elastic, and then up into the loop of the next stitch to the left, as shown.

Adding elastic to ribbing

When working with a non-resilient yarn such as cotton, you can knit in a matching elastic thread. But you can also add or replace elastic on completed knit pieces. Working from the wrong side of the ribbing, thread the elastic through the back of each knit stitch as shown and pull slightly to draw it in. Attach each elastic row to the side seams, keeping the same tension on all rows of elastic.

ZIPPERS

Several types of zippers can be added to knit garments. Heavier zippers that separate are used for jackets and cardigans. Regular dressmaking zippers are used for skirt waists or on the back of close-fitting necks.

Zippers should be sewn in by hand rather than by machine. The opening should be the same length as the zipper so that the seam doesn't stretch or pucker.

To prepare the edges of a garment for the zipper, work a selvage such as the two-stitch garter selvage. If the edge is not smooth enough, a crocheted slip stitch edge will be helpful.

Place the zipper in a stitch or two from the edge to prevent the teeth from showing, and sew it down with a backstitch.

ADDING A ZIPPER

Whip stitch the zipper in place on the wrong side, then backstitch it on the right side close to the edge of the knit fabric.

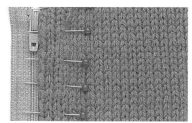

1 To apply the zipper, work from the right side of the piece or pieces with the zipper closed. Pin the zipper in place so that the edges of the knit fabric will cover the teeth of the zipper and meet in the center.

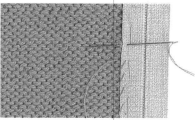

2 After pinning, baste the zipper and remove the pins. Turn the zipper to the wrong side and whip stitch in place. Turn the zipper to the right side and backstitch in place.

VIII. Embellishments

EMBROIDERY

Embroidery is used to add another dimension to your work once the knitting and blocking is complete. Embroidery is most effective on simple stitch patterns—stockinette stitch is the best.

Many types of yarn can be used for embroidery, but you should select one that is smooth enough to go through the knitted fabric. Make sure that the weight and content of the yarn is appropriate for the knit piece. Yarns that are too thin will sink into the fabric, and a too-thick yarn will stretch out the piece. The embroidery yarn should have the same care properties as the yarn used for your sweater and should be colorfast.

Back stitch is used for outlining and lines. Draw the needle up. In one motion, insert the needle a little behind where the yarn emerged and draw it up the same distance in front. Continue from right to left, by inserting the needle where the yarn first emerged.

Stem stitch is used for stems or outlining. Bring the needle up, then insert it a short distance to the right at an angle and pull it through. For stems, keep the thread below the needle. For outlines, keep the thread above the needle.

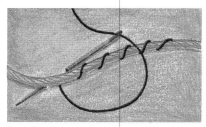

Couching is used to catch yarn laid on top of a knit piece. Place the yarn as desired, leaving a short strand at either end. Make stitches over the yarn as shown. To finish, thread the short strands and pull them through to the underside of the piece.

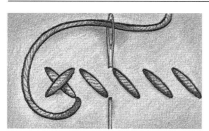

Cross stitch is a filling stitch. Pull the yarn through and make a diagonal stitch to the upper left corner. Working from right to left, make a parallel row of half cross stitches. Work back across the first set of diagonal stitches in the opposite direction, as shown.

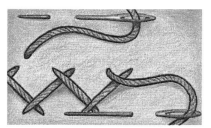

Herringbone stitch is used to hem, to fasten down facings, or as a filling stitch. Working from left to right, bring the needle up, then across diagonally and take a short stitch. Go down diagonally and take a short stitch.

Blanket or buttonhole stitch can be used to apply pieces such as pockets, to reinforce buttonholes, or for hemming. Bring the needle up. Keeping the needle above the yarn, insert it and bring it up again a short distance to the right, as shown. Pull the needle through to finish the stitch.

Complex patterns can be drawn on lightweight non-fusible interfacing and basted in place. Embroider over the interfacing and through the knit fabric. Cut away the interfacing once the pieces are complete. If the knitted fabric is lightweight, back the embroidery with a non-fusible interfacing on the wrong side of the work.

Work evenly and not too tightly, using a blunt needle with an eye large enough to accommodate the yarn but not so large that it will split the stitches. Thread the yarn by folding it around the needle and inserting the folded end into the eye. Do not knot the end of your yarn, but weave it through to the place where you will begin embroidering.

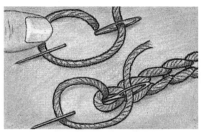

Chain stitch forms a line of chains for outlining or filling. Draw the needle up and *insert it back where it just came out, taking a short stitch. With the needle above the yarn, hold the yarn with your thumb and draw it through. Repeat from the *.

Lazy daisy stitch is used to make flowers. Work a chain stitch, but instead of going back into the stitch, insert the needle below and then above the stitch in one motion, as shown. Pull the needle through. Form new petals in the same way.

Satin stitch is ideal as a filling stitch. Be careful not to pull the stitches too tightly to avoid puckering. Bring the needle up at one side and insert it at an angle, covering the desired space in one motion. Repeat this step.

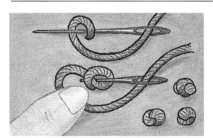

French knots can be used for flower centers, or they can be worked in bulky yarn to form rosettes. Bring the needle up and wrap the thread once or twice around it, holding the thread taut. Reinsert the needle at the closest point to where the thread emerged.

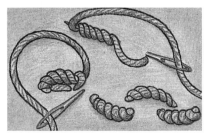

Bullion stitch is similar to French knots. Bring the needle up. Reinsert it as shown and wrap the yarn four to six times around it. Holding the yarn taut, pull the needle through. Reinsert the needle a short distance from where it emerged and pull it through.

Duplicate stitch covers a knit stitch. Bring the needle up below the stitch to be worked. Insert the needle under both loops one row above and pull it through. Insert it back into the stitch below and through the center of the next stitch in one motion, as shown.

Embroidery CONTINUED

Smocking

Smocking, or the honeycomb stitch, uses a ratio of three or four reverse stockinette stitches to one knit stitch, depending on the weight of yarn used. The fabric reduces approximately one-third when the smocking is complete. Run a contrasting yarn under the knit stitches to be smocked.

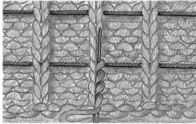

1 Beginning with the second knit rib at the lower right edge, bring the needle up the right side of that rib to the fourth stitch.

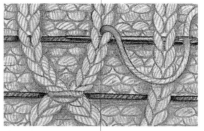

2 *Insert the needle from right to left into the fourth stitch (shown here after a few stitches have been smocked) of the first and second ribs. Bring the needle through and pull to join the ribs; repeat from the * once to complete a smocking stitch.

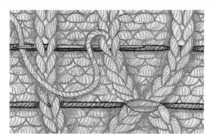

3 Bring the needle up the next four stitches on the left side of the second knit rib and work the smocking stitch, joining the second and third ribs by inserting the needle from left to right. Repeat steps 2 and 3 to the top of the piece.

Knitting with Beads

Knitting with beads is an age-old art that you can do in two ways. The first and easiest method, "beaded knitting," has beads spaced at planned or random intervals. The beads are added by threading them directly onto the working yarn. These beads usually fall over the stitches rather than between them. Beaded knitting is worked most often with one type or color of bead, but with advance planning as you thread, you can work out a sequence with several types or colors of beads. The techniques on the following page are for beaded knitting.

The second method, a traditional one first developed in the 18th and 19th centuries, was used for purses and other elaborately decorated items. It is called "bead knitting" (sometimes known as purse knitting). This method, also worked by threading the beads onto the working yarn, is done by placing one bead between each stitch, so that the knitting stitches are completely hidden by beads. You can work intricate patterns in bead knitting by threading beads in reverse of the design (which must be completely accurate) and then working the beads into the knitting.

Most beads are made from glass, wood, plastic, clay, and papier-mâché, but they can also be made from pearls, gems, buttons, and some stones. Match your beads to the yarn by using luxurious beads on silks and other shiny yarns for evening wear and rougher beads on tweeds and wools for day wear. When considering whether your beads and yarn are an appropriate match, remember that beads will add weight to your sweater. Heavy yarns with vast numbers of beads will not be comfortable to wear and are likely to stretch out. Fragile yarns should be beaded with care, because some are not strong enough to withstand the beading process without fraying or becoming worn. If your yarn is too thick to thread and bead, sew beads onto the finished pieces. When choosing suitable yarns and beads, make sure you can wash the beads if you are using a washable yarn. If you plan to dry clean the sweater, make sure the beads can be dry cleaned, too.

Work stitches firmly on either side of the beads to keep them in place and from falling to the back of the work. To avoid edges that curl or that are difficult to seam, don't work beads close to the edge of your pieces.

You can be creative when you add beads to stitch patterns. Add beads in pattern indentations, at the sides or centers of cables, or in the openings created by eyelet stitches.

Threading beads

For either beading method, thread beads onto balls of yarn before you knit. The threading needle must be large enough to accommodate the yarn, but small enough to go through the beads. Since this combination is not always possible, you can use an auxiliary thread to thread the beads. Using a sturdy thread, loop it through a folded piece of yarn and then pull both ends of the thread through the eye of the needle. Pass the bead over the needle and thread it onto the yarn. (It may help to pass a bead back and forth over the folded yarn a few times to crease it.)

Beads are available pre-strung or loose. Individual beads take longer to thread. To thread pre-strung beads, carefully open the strand and insert the needle into the beads through the strand. Store threaded beads in a

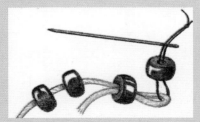

plastic bag or jar to keep them from tangling as you knit.

Knitting with Beads continued

Stockinette stitch

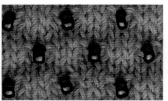

You can add beads in stockinette stitch on wrong-side rows by making a knit stitch (a purl on the right side of the work) on either side of the bead to help anchor it.

From the wrong side On a purl (wrong-side) row, work to one stitch before the point you wish to place a bead. Knit this stitch. With yarn still at back of the work, slip the bead up to the work and knit the next stitch.

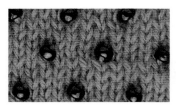

On right-side rows, beads are placed without the purl stitches on either side. The bead will lie directly in front of the stitch. Work the stitch firmly so that the bead won't fall to the back of the work.

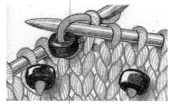

From the right side Work to the stitch to be beaded, then slip the bead up in back of the work. Insert needle as if to knit; wrap yarn around it. Push bead to front through the stitch on the left needle; complete the stitch.

Garter and reverse stockinette stitch

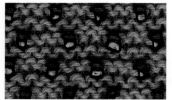

Add beads to garter stitch by working the wrong-side rows, so that the beads fall to the right side of the work. Work right-side rows with no beads.

Garter stitch With the yarn at the back, slip a bead close to the work, and then knit the next stitch from the left needle. The bead will sit between the two stitches.

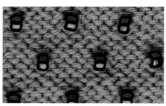

Beads can be added in reverse stockinette stitch on right-side (purl) rows.

Reverse stockinette stitch Work to the stitch where the bead will be placed; insert needle into next stitch as if to purl. Push the bead up to the front of the work; purl the stitch.

Slip stitch

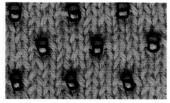

Adding beads with a slip stitch is done on stockinette stitch from the right side of the work. The bead falls directly in front of the slip stitch.

1 Work to where the bead is to be placed. Bring the yarn and the bead to the front of the work and slip the next stitch knitwise.

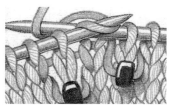

2 Bring the yarn to the back, keeping the bead to the front, and knit the next stitch firmly.

KNITTING WITH SEQUINS

Adding sequins is a glamorous way to embellish simple sweaters. As with beads, always work sequins a stitch or two in from the edges for easier seaming. Accuracy is important when you work with sequins, because they are difficult to rip out once knit.

Sequins come with holes at the top or in the center. The hole placement determines how the sequin will lie, which will affect the finished look of your sweater.

Special care may be needed for sequined garments. Some sequins can be hand washed but not dry cleaned. Sequins shouldn't be steamed or pressed. It's also a good idea to check them for colorfastness.

Thread sequins onto a ball of yarn before you begin, using an auxiliary thread. String shaped sequins onto the yarn with the cup side facing the ball, so that the cup, which has more facets, will face out once it is knit. Add enough sequins to knit a full ball of yarn.

STOCKINETTE STITCH

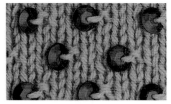

A purl stitch worked on one side of a sequin on stockinette stitch helps the sequin to lie flat. This is done on the right side (knit rows).

From the right side with a purl stitch Knit to the stitch where the sequin will be placed. Bring the yarn to the front and slide the sequin to the work. Purl the stitch.

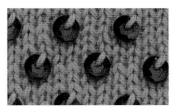

Adding sequins without a purl stitch on stockinette is more time consuming, but may be desirable for certain garments where the sequins must be anchored.

Without a purl stitch Work to where the sequin will be placed and insert the right needle into the back loop of the next stitch. Push the sequin close to the back of the work and then through the stitch with your finger.

GARTER AND REVERSE STOCKINETTE STITCH

When you work sequins into garter stitch on wrong-side rows, the sequin will fall between the two stitches on the right side of the work.

Garter stitch On the wrong-side row, work to where the sequin is to be placed and, with the yarn at the back, slip the sequin close to the work. Knit the next stitch, leaving the sequin between the two stitches.

Sequins can be worked on purl rows (the right side of reverse stockinette stitch).

Reverse stockinette stitch Work to placement of sequin. Twist the next stitch: slip it through the back loop and place it back on left needle. Push sequin close to work. Purl the twisted stitch, pushing sequin through.

ADDITIONS

Your sweater can be a base for adding a wide variety of creative extras. You can apply pieces of knit fabric, leather, or felt. You can also add ribbon, petals, purchased appliqués, cords, pompoms, tassels, beads, stones, or knit bobbles. Look in craft or millinery supply stores to find creative additions or make your own from the instructions that follow.

Additions such as ribbon, leather strips, and cord can be woven or laced into eyelets, lace stitches, loosely knit areas, or dropped-stitch spaces. You can create a plaid effect by weaving in strands of contrasting yarn.

Apply additions securely. They should not bind, pull, or pucker the knit fabric. If you plan to appliqué large areas, make sure that they will still have the same flexibility as the rest of the piece. Baste trims or additions to the sweater to check their placement before you attach them. Additions that need to be cleaned differently than your garment should be detachable.

CORDS

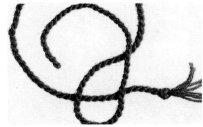

Twisted cord is made by twisting strands of yarn together. The thickness of the cord will depend on the number and weight of the strands. Cut strands three times the desired finished length and knot them about one inch (2.5cm) from each end.

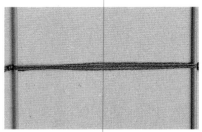

1 If you have someone to help you, insert a pencil or knitting needle through each end of the strands. If not, place one end over a doorknob and put a pencil through the other end. Turn the strands clockwise until they are tightly twisted.

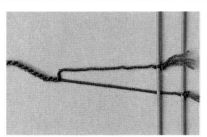

2 Keeping the strands taut, fold the piece in half. Remove the pencils and allow the cords to twist onto themselves.

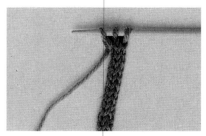

I-cord is made on double-pointed needles. Cast on about three to five stitches. *Knit one row. Without turning the work, slip the stitches back to the beginning of the row. Pull the yarn tightly from the end of the row. Repeat from the * as desired. Bind off.

FRINGES

Simple fringe Cut yarn twice the desired length plus extra for knotting. On the wrong side, insert the hook from front to back through the piece and over the folded yarn. Pull the yarn through. Draw the ends through and tighten. Trim the yarn.

Knotted fringe After working a simple fringe (it should be longer to account for extra knotting), take half of the strands from each fringe and knot them with half the strands from the neighboring fringe.

Knitted fringe This applied fringe is worked side to side. Cast on stitches to approximately one-fifth the desired length of the fringe. Work garter stitch to the desired width of the fringe band. Bind off four to five stitches.

Unravel remaining stitches to create the fringe, which may be left looped or cut. Apply the fringe to your garment at the garter stitch border.

TASSELS

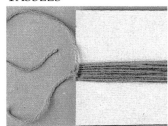

Tassel with shank Wrap yarn around a piece of cardboard that is the desired length of the tassel. Thread a strand of yarn, insert it through the cardboard, and tie it at the top, leaving a long end to wrap around the tassel.

Cut the lower edge to free the wrapped strands. Wrap the long end of the yarn around the upper edge and insert the yarn into the top, as shown. Trim the strands.

Tassel without shank Wrap yarn around cardboard the length of the tassel, leaving a 12-inch (30cm) strand loose at either end. With a yarn needle, knot both sides to the first loop and run the loose strand under the wrapped strands. Pull tightly and tie at the top.

Cut the lower edge of the tassel and, holding the tassel about three-fourths inch (2cm) from the top, wind the top strands (one clockwise and one counterclockwise) around the tassel. Thread the two strands and insert them through the top of the tassel.

POMPOMS

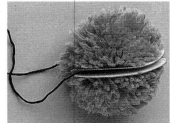

You can use pompoms as a decorative trim, at the ends of cords, on hats or hoods, and for children's garments. They are easy to make.

1 With two circular pieces of cardboard the width of the desired pompom, cut a center hole. Then cut a pie-shaped wedge out of the circle. Use the templates (see *Tables and Tools*) as guides.

2 Hold the two circles together and wrap the yarn tightly around the cardboard. Carefully cut around the cardboard.

3 Tie a piece of yarn tightly between the two circles. Remove the cardboard and trim the pompom.

Tables and Tools

Knitting needles

US	Metric
0	2mm
1	2.25mm
	2.5mm
2	2.75mm
	3mm
3	3.25mm
4	3.5mm
5	3.75mm
6	4mm
7	4.5mm
8	5mm
9	5.5mm
10	6mm
10 ½	6.5mm
	7mm
	7.5mm
11	8mm
13	9mm
15	10mm

Crochet hooks

US	Metric
14 steel	.60mm
12 steel	.75mm
10 steel	1.00mm
6 steel	1.50mm
5 steel	1.75mm
B/1	2.00mm
C/2	2.50mm
D/3	3.00mm
E/4	3.50mm
F/5	4.00mm
G/6	4.50mm
H/8	5.00mm
I/9	5.50mm
J/10	6.00mm
	6.50mm
K/10 1/2	7.00mm

SUBSTITUTING YARNS

Sometimes the yarn specified in a pattern or the yarn you had in mind for a design is not available, and you need to make a substitution. Substituting yarn is not simply a matter of replacing one ball for another, even when they are the same weight or length. It is also difficult to substitute one texture for another. The only way to make sure the substitution is accurate is to knit a swatch and compare its gauge with the gauge given for the original yarn.

After you've successfully gauge-swatched a substitute yarn, you'll need to figure out how much of the substitute yarn the project requires. First, find the total length of the original yarn in the pattern (multiply number of balls by yards/meters per ball). Divide this figure by the new yards/meters per ball (listed on the yarn label). Round up to the next whole number. The answer is the number of balls required.

Conversion chart

MULTIPLY	BY	TO GET
Cms	0.394	Inches
Grams	0.035	Ounces
Inches	2.54	Cms
Yards	.91	Meters

Equivalent weights

¾oz = 20g	1¾ oz = 50g
1 oz = 28g	2 oz = 60g
1½oz = 40g	3 oz = 100g

Needle Inventory

US	0	1		2		3	4	5	6	7
mm	2	2.25	2.5	2.75	3	3.25	3.5	3.75	4	4.5
Straight										
Circular										
Double-pointed										

US	8	9	10	10½			11	13	15	17
mm	5	5.5	6	6.5	7	7.5	8	9	10	12.75
Straight										
Circular										
Double-pointed										

POMPOM TEMPLATE

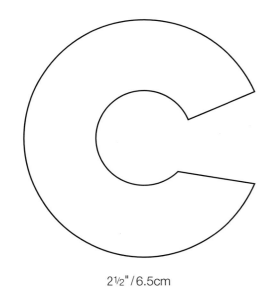

2½" / 6.5cm

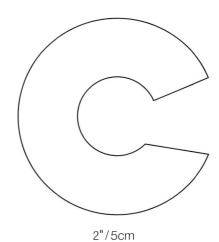

2" / 5cm

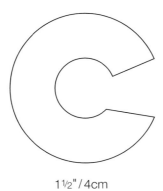

1½" / 4cm

NOTES

NOTES

NOTES

Notes

NOTES

ACKNOWLEDGMENTS

Thanks to Susan Levin of K1C2, without whom the idea of compiling a compendium to the ever-popular *Vogue® Knitting* reference book might not have come to be. In a conversation with editor-in-chief Trisha Malcolm, Susan said, "I never remember how to make a one-row buttonhole without looking it up. Wouldn't it be great to have a portable version of the *Vogue Knitting* Book?" So the editors of "VK", some new and some who worked on the very first publication, spent many painstaking hours coming up with a comprehensive knitting guide that is portable and features the best of the original book.

We are forever indebted to the original team of editors, knitters, illustrators, graphic artists, designers, and photographers who willingly took on the enormous task of creating *Vogue® Knitting: The Ultimate Knitting Book.* Without their tenacity, knowledge, dedication, and devotion we would never have the wonderful resource that has become the guidebook of our knitting lives. Special thanks to those who worked tirelessly on this new version to ensure its accuracy and make it simple to follow for all knitters.

128